Cupcakery

Praise for *Cupcakery*

"Toni Miller's *Cupcakery* is filled with colorful cupcake confections! Her nostalgic and crowd-pleasing cupcake recipes are great for parties or just as a fun treat for your loved one."

— *Amy Atlas*
bestselling author of *Sweet Designs*

"Toni Miller brings a fun creativity to cupcakes that makes me want to smile from ear to ear. The designs and recipes are flawless and easy to execute with her detailed instructions. Everyday is a better day with *Cupcakery*!"

— *Amanda Rettke*
author of *Surprise-Inside Cakes* and baker/blogger behind iambaker.net

"*Cupcakery* is the perfect addition to any hostess's bookshelf! It's filled with dozens of fabulous ideas for dazzling cupcakes that are perfect for every celebration!"

— *Courtney Whitmore*
author of *Push-Up Pops, Candy Making for Kids,* and *Frostings*

"From the moment I laid eyes on Toni's adorable cupcake creations, I was insanely inspired! From her mouth-watering and easy-to-follow recipes to her creative and colorful designs, the book provides incredibly fun and imaginative ideas for any birthday, holiday, or special celebration! Toni's detailed instructions make the book a must-have for bakers of all skill levels, with tips and techniques to help each step of the way! *Cupcakery* is not only a feast for the eyes, but most definitely for the sweet-craving stomach as well!"

— *Lynlee North Beckett*
author of *Sweet & Unique Toppers*

"*Cupcakery* is packed with scrumptious recipes and colorful creative flair, but the real icing on the (cup)cake is its approachability! Toni does an incredible job of presenting each idea in a clear-cut manner that makes stylish baking accessible and fun."

— *Jennifer Sbranti*
founder and editor-in-chief of Hostess with the Mostess

"With easy-to-follow recipes and bright, colorful presentation ideas, *Cupcakery* will make your next batch the hit of the party!"

— *Callye Alvarado*
author of *The Sweet Adventures of Sugarbelle*

PARTY-PERFECT CUPCAKES IN A FLASH

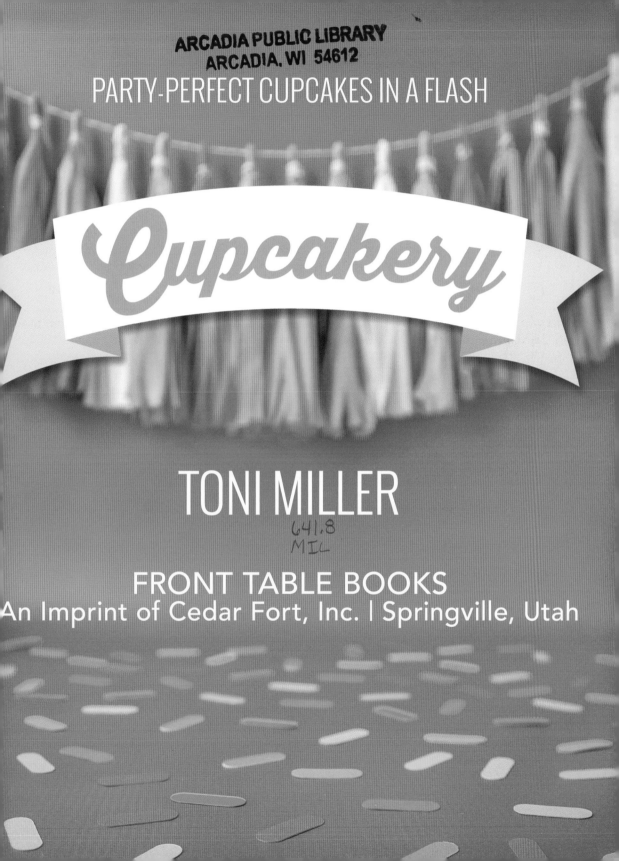

Cupcakery

TONI MILLER

FRONT TABLE BOOKS
An Imprint of Cedar Fort, Inc. | Springville, Utah

ISBN 13: 978-1-4621-1626-3

Published by Front Table Books, an imprint of Cedar Fort, Inc.
2373 W. 700 S., Springville, UT 84663
Distributed by Cedar Fort, Inc., www.cedarfort.com

LIBRARY OF CONGRESS CATALOGING-IN-PUBLICATION DATA

Miller, Toni, 1987-
Cupcakery / Toni Miller.
      pages cm
Includes index.
ISBN 978-1-4621-1626-3
1. Cupcakes. I. Title.

TX771.M455 2015
641.8'653--dc23
                      2015001659

Cover design by Lauren Error
Page design by Lauren Error and Michelle May
Cover design © 2015 by Lyle Mortimer
Edited by Sydnee Hyer

Printed in United States

10 9 8 7 6 5 4 3 2 1

Printed on acid-free paper

To my three sweet cupcakes,
Cadence, Miley, and Bailey.

Contents

The Sweet Life

I would love to begin by telling you that I grew up in a bakery,

surrounded by cakes, cupcakes, and the smell of fresh cookies daily. And I wish I could assure you that Candy Land is a real place, that calories don't count in dessert, and that I was frosting mile-high cupcakes by the age of three. But the truth is that, aside from the occasional holiday baking, most of my childhood baked-good memories come from the local bakery. The extent of my baking knowledge was a boxed cake, frosted from a can. Barely legible writing, sprinkles, and matching candles earned extra cool points. Becoming a baker was nowhere near my list of things I wanted to be when I grew up.

While I may not have been raised by Willy Wonka or been a child prodigy in cake decorating, life was still pretty sweet. From the start, it was pretty clear I had a creative drive and an undeniable sweet tooth. I was always surrounded by lots of family who embraced my creative nature, no matter how much glitter stuck to the kitchen table. As I grew older, I found one of my favorite ways to use those gifts was to plan themed events and entertain guests, a hobby that followed me into adulthood. Soon after marrying my high school sweetheart and having our first baby girl, I had the best reason to throw adorably cute birthday parties. We were a traveling military family, and big parties were a wonderful way to bring new friends together. You could say that's where my baking journey began, because every party needs a cake.

> **Becoming a baker was nowhere near my list of things I wanted to be when I grew up.**

As I'm sure you already know, party cakes today are quite different from the past. Today, you will find that cake decorating has progressed from using a star tip and a molded pan to carving real-life edible sculptures. Cakes come in all shapes and sizes—there's no limit to the creativity—and I wanted my party cakes to be the centerpiece! Unfortunately, it seemed that after spending weeks planning every single detail of a party, I would pick up the cake and find myself incredibly disappointed, cake fail after cake fail. The very last cake I ever ordered was for my daughter's second birthday. We picked up our requested pink and purple cake only to find a cake that was half purple and half pink with a dividing line drawn right down the center. Just as we set down our two-toned cake, it split right

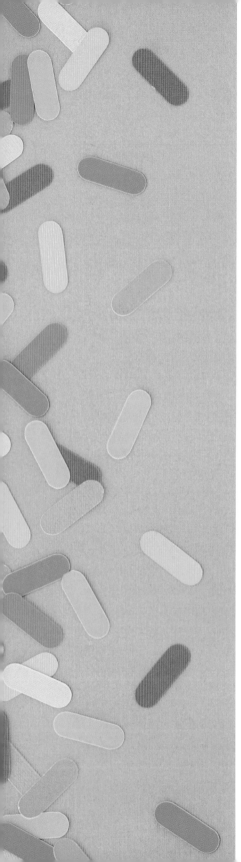

down the center. Of course, it's not that all bakers or bakeries produce awful cakes, but we certainly had a bad run, for which I'm now thankful! Those disappointing cake fails led me right to the sweet life.

Seeing my frustration, my incredible husband encouraged me to start baking and decorating cakes of my own. A trip to the local craft store, one giant decorating kit, and a few practice cakes later, I was hooked. I adored the art of not only baking but also decorating cakes. Before I knew it, I was making cake after cake for friends and friends of friends. But the more full my cake calendar got, the less I enjoyed making them. I was filling cake requests and spending my weekends covered in buttercream instead of being creative and spending time with my family, who at that time consisted of a soldier husband, an energetic toddler, and newborn twins. Somewhere in the mix I started baking cupcakes, the smaller-yet-just-as-yummy-and-more-adorable sister to cakes. I quickly discovered I could be just as creative with cupcakes, maybe even more so. I could easily change the flavor, frosting color, and cupcake liner print, add a surprise inside, or top with anything from simple candies to extravagant fondant toppers. And I could perfectly coordinate the cupcakes with any event or occasion I could dream up! My love for cupcakes had just begun and I had no idea of the sweet adventures they would lead me to.

Soon, I began whipping up cupcakes in every flavor you could imagine. I shared my sugary creations with friends and neighbors. Quickly I became the cupcake lady, and I was more than happy with that role. As I shifted my focus from the art of decorating cakes to the science of baking and developing new flavor combos, my recipes were requested more and more. I firmly believe that recipes should be shared and I have been more than willing to hand over any recipe I have created. But much like great recipes, time is precious. I found myself typing out the same recipes and the same information over and over again.

This, my friends, is where all the fun begins—in the creative corners of the Internet, the blogosphere. During my own quest to perfect my art of baking and decorating, I found out that there are websites and blogs completely dedicated to all things sweet! Cookies, cakes, cupcakes, lollipops, you name it—there were enthusiasts out there sharing their love of sweets with the world, and I wanted a slice! I knew starting a blog would be the perfect way to share recipes and tutorials with family and friends around the world, to continue to connect and share my love of baking and decorating party sweets no matter where the military sent us. What I didn't know is that silly little blog would become much more than a place to store my recipes. Soon it began to grow, and I was gaining readers around the world, far outside my circle of family and friends. I had found my spot, with no messy faces or official orders, where I could be creative, bake sweet treats, have fun, and show others how to do it too! Soon I began exploring and sharing not only cupcakes and cakes but practically any party-worthy treat. I began to share much more than just recipes. I had set out to share a love of sweets with bakers, mothers, entertainers, and more. I strived to share party-perfect treats that were just as cute as they were delicious and show readers that they could make them too! Today, thanks to my incredible readers, family, and friends, each day is an exciting, sprinkle-covered adventure. I never know what I will be creating next—and I wouldn't have it any other way.

No matter where my frosted adventure has taken me, cupcakes have and will always have a special place in my heart. No matter how many cupcakes I bake or parties I throw, I just can't get enough of them! My hope for this little book is to share that love with all of you. Because I promise that everybody can make party-perfect cupcakes without a trip to the bakery or a culinary degree. Within this book you will find 50 adorably sweet, party-perfect cupcake recipes and all my cupcake tricks and tips from baking to packaging. I've combined easy and creative recipes with bright and simple styling to fit any event, from everyday occasions to holiday celebrations. Each and every recipe has been created to not only taste and look great, but also have you in and out of the kitchen with plenty of time for the party.

No, it's not magic; it's . . .

cupcakery!

Cupcakes 101

From supplies to the sugar on top, I'll guide you through tips, tricks, and basics of creating the most adorably delicious cupcakes.

Cupcake Tools

*S*ometimes the difference between success and disaster in a craft is simply a matter of having the right tools. Cupcake baking is no different; having the right tools on hand not only increases your chances of sweet success, but it also makes the process much easier as a whole. I won't deny I absolutely love shopping for new baking supplies. I have an entire drawer full of spatulas! But the truth is, no matter how many incredibly cute and handy baking supplies you can find, party-perfect cupcakes can be created with just a few simple and easy-to-find tools that you may even already own. Below, you can find the most common supplies I use throughout *Cupcakery* and in my own kitchen.

STAND MIXER/ELECTRIC MIXER—While you certainly can whip up cupcakes by hand—and get a workout in while you're at it—you won't want to tackle frosting with a whisk. You're going to need a little more power to get that light and fluffy frosting we all know and love. I use my stand mixer for the most part, but a good electric hand mixer will do just fine, if necessary. I personally recommend investing in a quality stand mixer if you do a lot of baking and cooking. When I first began my adventures in baking, I went through cheap hand mixers like disposable piping bags. The day I brought home my first KitchenAid stand mixer was a day to remember, for sure! Not only did the quality of my treats improve, but the process became much easier and I began finding everyday uses for it.

MEASURING TOOLS—Most of us already have these in our kitchen. But if not, you're going to need a full set of measuring cups, tablespoons, and teaspoons. I'd also recommended keeping a small liquid measuring cup on hand; they are useful when it comes to adding fluid to frostings.

SPATULAS—I promise you really don't need an entire drawer of spatulas! I do recommend, however, keeping two types of spatulas around for baking cupcakes: a large one to scrape bowls and transfer frosting and a small one to measure out batter. The little spatulas with soft silicone tips are one of my favorite baking tools. These can often be found in sets of two on store endcaps and in seasonal baking sections.

CUPCAKE PANS—Also known as muffin pans, at least one of these can be found in most everyone's kitchen. When baking cupcakes, I would recommend having at least two on hand to make your process go faster, since most recipes will yield at least 24 cupcakes. Don't stress about purchasing the absolute best-quality pans for the recipes in this book. Most cake mixes are developed to bake even in average bakeware you would find in just about any home. I love to use Wilton's non-stick steel muffin pans. They are great quality and affordable, and they look the same as the day I purchased them, several thousand cupcakes later!

CUPCAKE LINERS AND BAKING CUPS—Cupcake liners have came a long way from the standard pastel and foil packs sold in the grocery stores of the past. As the decorated-desserts trend grows, so does the variety of cupcake liners—the fashion of cupcakes, if you will. No matter how many options are available, there is nothing worse than picking out the cutest cupcake liners and baking your cupcakes, only to realize the print and color have completely faded with the moisture in the cake. Polka dots and ladybugs just aren't as cute saturated in oil. Thankfully, we now have options. A few years ago, I discovered greaseproof cupcake liners and have never turned back. My favorite greaseproof cupcake liners, which you will see throughout the book, are from an online shop: Sweets and Treats Boutique. Not only do they hold up to the darkest of chocolate cakes, but they also hold their shape perfectly. Be cautious of buying cupcake liners in the store, as most of them will fade when baked, though greaseproof is becoming more and more common. You can also find foil-lined cupcake papers, which also hold their shape well but do sacrifice some quality when bent or pinched. Another option I like are sturdy greaseproof baking cups, which I often find at discount stores like Homegoods or Ross. These cups allow you to bake without even using a pan and hold up to their greaseproof claim. However, cupcakes tend to bake unevenly in them, so I prefer to first bake them in a good cupcake liner and then place them inside the baking cups just

BAKER'S TIP

Craft and hobby stores carry a large selection of baking and decorating supplies. They have frequent sales and coupons to purchase items at a discounted price.

afterward for display (see Caramel Popcorn, page 77). Cupcake wraps are another option for dressing up a cupcake. These are most often found online and come in a flat pack that needs to be set up and placed around a baked cupcake (see Strawberry Princess, page 66, for an example). If you're up for a project, with a quick online search you can also find templates to print and cut your own themed wrappers.

CUPCAKE CORER—These are optional, but they can be a handy tool. They help carve out a little hollow spot in the cupcake to fill with something yummy, but you can achieve the same result without one. One trick I often use is to use the large open end of a frosting tip (see Coring & Filling, page 17). A small teaspoon will also get the job done.

GEL COLORINGS—Sometimes cupcakes need a little splash of color, or should I say a little *gel* of color! Unless you're accustomed to decorating desserts, you may not know that there are several types of food colorings available. Most homes are familiar with the small liquid bottles from the grocery store, but those are often the culprits behind frosting fails. The liquid isn't strong enough to achieve the desired color in a frosting or cake. By the time you've added enough coloring, your frosting has become runny and is still not quite the shade you were expecting. Gel coloring is much more functional for baking and decorating cupcakes. Not only does it allow for a more vibrant color with less liquid, it also comes in an endless assortment of colors. You can find gel coloring in almost any cake decorating section, sold by the color. The two brands I use most often are Wilton and AmeriColor. You will notice I do not list a specific amount of coloring in any of the recipes. This is because, unlike liquid drops, there's really no way to measure how much to use. It's always best to start with a small amount and add more if necessary. A pea-size amount of coloring can easily color a whole batch of frosting; a little goes a long way. You will quickly get the hang of how much you like to use. Keep in mind that coloring will get darker once baked or after sitting overnight in frosting.

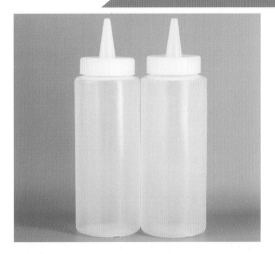

PIPING BAGS—Piping bags are one of the two essential tools for decorating cupcakes with frosting. They come in a variety of sizes and types, from disposable to cloth. I personally like to use 12- to 15-inch disposable clear bags, which can be found in almost any cake decorating section. They are especially great for beginners. In a pinch, a large Ziploc bag can be used.

PIPING TIPS—Piping tips are the second essential tool in cupcake decorating. While your piping bag will hold your frosting in place, you will need a tip to actually form the frosting into those sweet swirls. Some of the most common tips I use are Wilton 1M, 2D, and 2A. You can create endless styles of cupcake creations with just these three tips! Find more information on the tips I have used in this book on page 23.

DECORATING BOTTLES—Decorating bottles are not a necessity for all cupcake recipes, but they come in handy when working with liquids to top or fill cupcakes with, such as syrup or caramel (see Green Velvet Butterscotch, page 101). They contain the liquid better, creating much less mess and giving more piping control. The bottles are inexpensive and can be found in just about any store that has a cake-decorating section.

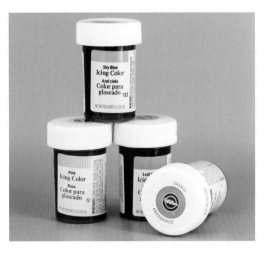

Ingredients & Supplies

When I first began my baking adventure, I was adamant that all of my treats needed to be from scratch. How could I call myself a baker otherwise? Fast forward a few years and I've learned that, just like everything else, baking has many different paths that all lead to the same result: a sweet memory and a delicious treat to share and enjoy. Sometimes I enjoy baking from scratch, right down to the homemade vanilla. But other times baking from a cake mix is exactly what I need! I soon began to find ways to adapt cake mixes, keeping them easy but making them even more delicious. With a few adaptations I could create treats that were bakery fresh but had the stability of a cake mix. Then I began to experiment with fun and creative frosting flavors made from all kinds of flavorings. Below I'll explain the recurring ingredients you will find within the book that have become cupcake staples in my kitchen.

CAKE MIX—Cake mixes are specifically created to make worry-free cakes, each of which can easily be turned into cupcakes. Unlike a from-scratch recipe that can be ruined with a small error, cake mixes are harder to mess up. Using a cake mix will take out the guesswork and fear. You will be amazed at how easy it is to turn a cake mix into a bakery-style cake with just a few alternative or additional ingredients!

INSTANT PUDDING—It may sound odd, but instant pudding is one of my favorite ingredients to spruce up a cupcake in more ways than one. A simple addition of instant pudding in a cake batter can help give the cake more moisture, flavor, density, and even rise! Sometimes cake mixes come packaged with "pudding in the mix," but don't worry; a little more pudding won't hurt. In addition to adding pudding inside the cake batter, prepared pudding makes the perfect cupcake filling. You'll notice that the cake recipes within the book will call for 4 tablespoons of instant pudding mix, which is half of a 3.4-ounce box of instant pudding. Be sure to hang on to the other half for future cupcake recipes. When instant pudding is called for in an ingredient list, it is always in its dry mix form.

EGGS—Eggs play a huge role in cake, having an impact on the moisture, leaving, tenderness, and binding. As you're probably well aware, eggs come in multiple sizes. You will find I use large eggs in the recipes. While the wrong egg size won't generally destroy your cupcakes, too much or too little egg can definitely alter the end result. They may make the cake fall apart or the texture too tough. Here's an easy chart to help you substitute other egg sizes you may already have on hand.

Medium—add ½ egg
Extra Large—reduce ½ egg
Jumbo—reduce 1 egg

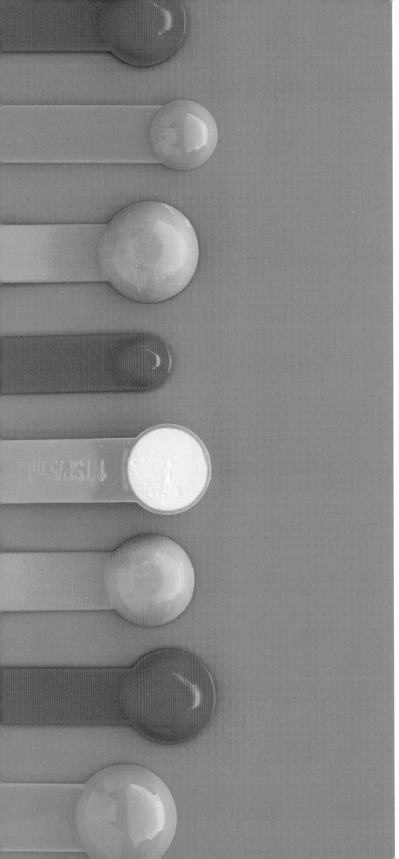

BAKER'S TIP

Yogurt and mayonnaise
are great substitutions
for sour cream
when needed.

SOUR CREAM—Sour cream is another ingredient you may wonder why on earth I'm using in cake mix. While there are many great attributes to using sour cream in cake mixes, the main reason I use sour cream is to add even more moisture to the cake. Because sour cream is a middle ground between a liquid and a solid, it allows us to add more fat to the cake without risking—and even improving—the structure of the cake by adding too much liquid. Yogurt and mayonnaise are great substitutions for sour cream when needed.

MILK—Most of us already have milk in our fridge. I use milk in place of water in my recipes to once again increase the moisture in the cake, due to the fat. For this reason, I use 2% or whole milk if possible. While the latter does give more moisture to the cake, the difference is subtle, so don't stress about the fat content of the milk you have on hand, though I would stay away from skim milk. Some recipes, such as "velvets," call for buttermilk. If necessary, you can make your own buttermilk by adding 1 tablespoon of white vinegar to 1 cup of milk and letting it sit for 20 minutes.

BUTTER—Bring on the butter! Every recipe in this book will call for butter. It's important to notice the difference between salted vs. unsalted and real butter vs. margarine sticks. For these recipes, you will need to pick up real butter, unsalted if possible. If you have salted on hand, don't be afraid to use it, but it's important to know the reason I use unsalted butter instead of salted butter. It's because I can then control the salt content in the recipe. I love the creamy soft taste of buttercreams made with unsalted butter. It's easy to add salt to a recipe to tone down a bit of sweetness, but it's impossible to remove it. I also use butter as a liquid fat in each cake batter in place of oil, which increases the moisture in the final result. You will also notice I do not specifically call for unsalted butter in the cakes because it really doesn't make a difference.

SHORTENING—Shortening is often the center of great debate in baking. Some people really dislike the use of shortening in their recipes, and that's okay. However, I prefer to use it in buttercreams. Shortening, when used in frostings, gives the frosting more stability, makes it easier to work with, and gives it a whiter color. It also has a higher melting point, which comes in handy when baking treats in warm temperatures that may otherwise melt, such as an outdoor party or event. When purchasing shortening, I always buy quality shortenings. If you would really rather not use shortening in your frosting, feel free to substitute it with butter (but double the amount). Just know that the frosting will not be as stable.

FLAVORING—There are endless options when it comes to flavoring ingredients. I love to create fun and festive flavors with simple food items we often use. The most common items I use to flavor cupcakes in this book are extracts, candy flavorings, puddings, juices, and even drink mixes. All of the flavorings in this book were found at local grocery, craft, or baking stores. If there is ever a flavoring you can't seem to find in stores, you can definitely find it with a quick search online.

BAKER'S TIP

8 cups of powdered sugar is equal to one 2-pound bag.

SUGAR—Sugar is definitely not in short supply here! You will find the most-used sugar in this book is powdered sugar, also known as confectioner's sugar. My only real guidance here is to stay away from off-brands if at all possible. I often find frostings made with off-brand sugars have more grit to them, which of course can result in a gritty frosting. Many recipes will call for 8 cups of powdered sugar, which is the same as one 2-pound bag.

Baked to Perfection

*B*aking, no matter what level, is a science. Whether you realize it or not, everything you bake is the result of a chemical reaction that occurs the moment that ingredients are combined. This is why baking can be so tricky and often frustrating when outcomes vary. Even though these recipes are really easy to use and hard to mess up, we're human, so there's room for error. But don't worry, I won't get too geeky on you. I've spent a great deal of time obsessing over every little detail that baking cupcakes requires to make the process easier and with great outcomes. Here, I'll go into more details of my baking process outside of just the recipes, for those of you who don't want to miss a trick!

PREP—One of the best things you can do to improve your cupcakes is to take the time to prepare for your project. It will speed up the process and make it more enjoyable. I like to read over the recipe once and then measure and prepare all the ingredients while the oven is preheating. There's really nothing worse than finding out your milk magically walked away mid-recipe. Also, I typically melt any butter, if needed, first so it has time to cool.

MIXING—Mixing the batter is a really important step in baking cupcakes, and often the most underestimated step. Mixing not only combines ingredients, but it also adds air to the cake batter. Both undermixing and overmixing can be fatal. I often recommend mixing all the ingredients on low until combined, taking time to scrape the bottom of the bowl with a spatula to make sure no ingredients are left unmixed, and then turning the mixer up to medium for 15 seconds, making sure not to overmix. Gummy cupcake tops are a sign of poorly mixed cupcakes.

BAKER'S TIP

Sifting dry ingredients helps break down all the little clumps that can accumulate in your ingredients from sitting. If you don't have a sifter on hand, a large strainer will do the trick. Just shake and tap it on the side of the bowl. If you have lots of little clumps left, break them up by pushing them through the bottom of the strainer or sifter with a spatula.

MEASURING BATTER—When it comes to measuring cupcake batter, I'm a bit obsessive compulsive. I like to measure my batter to make sure my cupcakes are going to bake nice and consistent. I almost always measure out three level tablespoons into each liner, using a small silicone spatula to scrape and level. If the thought of measuring out three

BAKER'S TIP

To turn any of these recipes into mini cupcakes, use 1 tablespoon of batter in each mini liner.

tablespoons for every cupcake is a bit much for you, no worries. There are a few other options to help keep them consistent, like using a small ice cream or cookie dough scoop, or slightly less than a ¼ cup. Just before baking, tap the cupcake pan on the counter a couple of times to remove excess air bubbles and help the batter settle.

BAKING—Once you've placed your cupcake pans in the oven, there's not a whole lot you can do, but there are a few things you *shouldn't* do. It's really important not to open the oven door for at least the first 10 minutes, avoiding it altogether if possible. Most of the chemical reactions will take place the first few minutes in the oven, and opening the door will cause a sudden drop in temperature and disrupt that process, often causing the cake to fall. Another baking complication you want to avoid is overloading your oven. I bake all of my cupcakes in the center of the oven one cupcake pan at a time, filling the second tray while the first is baking. I feel that cupcakes like to have the center stage and they turn out their absolute best when baked on their own. If you're not quite as picky as me or you're short on time,

feel free to bake two 12-cup pans together side by side in the center of the oven for the most uniform results. If the recipe yields more than 24 cupcakes, wait for the first two trays to come out before baking any more. The last and most important baking mistake you can make is overbaking your cupcakes. Most of my cupcakes bake successfully between 16 and 18 minutes, depending on temperature, cake batter, and pan thickness. As soon as a toothpick comes out clean or the top of your cupcake springs back when touched, they are ready.

REMOVING & COOLING—Once the cupcakes are done, place the pan on the counter and let them sit for 2–4 minutes. Cupcakes fresh from the oven are still fragile and will damage easily. After a few moments, use a toothpick, fork, or small metal spatula to gently lift the cupcakes from the pan and place on a cooling rack. The cooling rack allows the hot air to escape instead of trapping too much moisture in the bottom. Allow the cupcakes to cool completely before coring or frosting, normally about 20 minutes. This is the perfect time to tidy up your work area and make your frosting.

BAKER'S TIP

When separating cupcake liners, separate the original stack into smaller stacks and push the bottom liner off the stack with your thumb, continuing up from the bottom. This will keep their shape instead of pulling out the top liners and bending the shape. Place the liners in the cavities, but do not push down; let the weight of the batter pull the liner down into place.

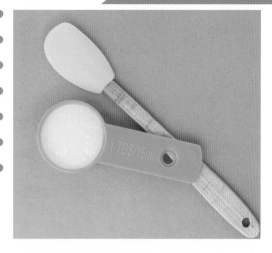

BAKER'S TIP

Quickly core a cupcake using
a large piping tip.

CORING & FILLING—Filling a cupcake is simple and really takes a cupcake to the next level. To fill a cupcake, you want to make sure your cupcake is completely cooled first. Warm cupcakes are less stable and more likely to tear if cored too soon. To core, you have a few options to chose from. Use a cupcake corer, piping tip, teaspoon, or small knife to hollow out a small spot right in the center of the cupcake, about ¾ inch to 1 inch deep. While you're coring the cupcakes, set each centerpiece in front of the cupcake it goes with so you can place it back on once filled, if you would like. Fill a piping bag or decorating bottle with your filling and, placing the tip down inside the cupcake, apply pressure and pull up. Fill until the filling is just below the top of the cupcake. Replace the cupcake center back on top and gently push down into place. If the filling is thick, you can fill right to the top and frost right on top. If you are using a really thin filling, like caramel (see Chocolate Caramel Irish Cream, page 102), you can skip the coring completely by using a tip specifically made for filling. After filling the piping bag, place the tip halfway down into the center of the cupcake, apply pressure, and then pull up while decreasing pressure. If any filling can be seen on top, simply scrape it off with a knife before frosting.

The Frosting on Top

This is where the real fun begins! Don't get me wrong; cake is great, but the frosting is where it's at! The frosting on a cupcake is what really separates cupcakes from cakes. Cupcakes don't rely on frosting for structure or stability as cakes do, so you can get even more creative with flavors and types. Making frosting is simple, and even if you make mistakes, they can usually be fixed. The reason frosting is one of my favorite parts is because it truly allows me to get creative. There are endless flavor and decorative possibilities to take your cupcake to a whole new level, no matter the occasion. From the surprise filling in the center to the sweet swirl on top, let's talk about how to get creative in the kitchen.

BAKER'S TIP

For a smoother, less grainy frosting, sift dry ingredients or send them through the food processor.

BEATING & COMBINING—While the ingredients will vary, you will find it's the same overall process for creating each type within *Cupcakery*. I've shared many easy-to-use recipes that only require the beating and combining (mixing) of ingredients. Unlike cake batter, you can't really overmix frostings.

You will start by beating butter at medium-high until soft and smooth. Ideally, you should leave the butter out on the counter to soften a bit when prepping your ingredients; however, if you forget, simply cut up the butter into small cubes before beating. It will take a little bit longer, but you will be able to bring it to the right consistency. When it comes to frostings, I actually prefer that the butter remain a bit cold and not come to room temperature because it's much easier to work with. Once your butter has had a good beating, add in your next solid or fat if listed, such as shortening or cream cheese. Beat on medium again until combined. Once your solids have been combined, turn your mixer down to low and slowly add in powdered sugar and any other dry ingredients, like cocoa, beating in between each addition. Once all of your dry ingredients have been added, you can increase your mixer speed until everything is nice and combined (frosting may appear crumbly at this point).

BAKER'S TIP

If filling contains fruit pieces that will clog the filling tip, place filling in blender and puree until filling is thin enough to pass through the tip.

FLAVORING & COLOR—Flavoring can be done in two parts of the recipe. It is generally combined with the fats; however, if you feel that the flavor just isn't as strong as you would like after combining the powdered sugar, you can go ahead and add a little more. If coloring the frostings using

gel colors (page 8), it should be done just after adding the powdered sugar and a small amount of liquid. You want to make sure you have brought the frosting to the desired color before adding the remaining liquid because even gel coloring can change the consistency of frostings, especially in strong colors where a lot is needed. It's important to note that coloring does often strengthen after several hours, so it's always best to stop one shade lighter than your desired outcome. When flavoring and adding color to frostings, you can keep the mixture at a low speed.

BAKER'S TIP

If your frosting is ready but your cupcakes are not, place a damp paper towel over the frosting bowl to help keep the frosting from drying out. Re-whip it just before using.

CONSISTENCY—Consistency is perhaps the most important step in making frosting for cupcakes. Once all other ingredients have been added, it's time to bring your frosting to consistency by adding your final wet ingredient, which often consists of milk but can be replaced with juices, creamers, and so on. Once the wet ingredient(s) have been completely combined, give your frosting one last good whip on medium high to make sure it's nice and fluffy. The perfect frosting consistency depends on the type of frosting you're making and what tip you're using. It may take a bit of practice before you know what you like the best. Buttercream tends to be on the thick side and holds up well when frosted with any tip if not overmoistened, especially if shortening is used in the recipe. Other softer, more temperamental frostings, like cream cheese or whipped cream, will need less moisture added to them. Too much moisture in softer frostings will make them hard to work with, and they can potentially sink when frosted. The great thing about making frosting is if you ever feel like you've added too much of the wet ingredients, you can slowly add a little more powdered sugar to bring it back to a firmer consistency.

EXTRA FROSTING – When it comes to frosting, my policy is you can never have too much! You may find that the frosting recipes in this book produce a lot of frosting. I like to make large batches of frosting so I have room for error. If I want to "refrost" a few cupcakes I can scrape them off and restart without worry. It's hard to really say what the perfect amount of frosting is because each person will frost cupcakes differently. I tend to pile mine on nice and tall. It's much better to have more than you need than not enough; nobody wants a naked cupcake. If you tend to like small amounts of frosting, feel free to cut any frosting recipe in half. But if you do have extra, don't toss it right away. Instead make cookie or graham cracker sandwiches or save it for a later use, like for cake pops.

STORING – Many frostings will store nicely in the fridge. While cream cheese frostings will only last a few days, buttercreams can actually be stored in the fridge for up to two weeks. Before using the frosting, you will need to remove it from the fridge to let it warm up just a bit and then whip it again before piping. You may also need to add a little more milk (or alternate fluid) to get it back to the proper consistency. You can even store buttercreams in an airtight container in the freezer for up to three months. Just place it in the fridge the day before to soften and repeat the steps listed above just before using.

If you're looking for a simple buttercream for a creation of your own, here are my favorite vanilla and chocolate buttercreams to both frost and decorate with.

VANILLA BUTTERCREAM

1 cup unsalted butter

1 cup shortening

1 Tbsp. clear vanilla extract

8 cups powdered sugar

6–8 Tbsp. milk

In the bowl of a stand mixer (or a large mixing bowl) using the paddle attachment, cream butter at medium speed until soft and smooth. Add shortening and extract and beat until combined. Slowly add in powdered sugar, beating slightly between each addition. Add milk one tablespoon at a time, beating in between additions until at desired consistency. Turn mixer up to medium-high and beat for 1–2 minutes.

CHOCOLATE BUTTERCREAM

1 cup unsalted butter

1 cup shortening

1 Tbsp. vanilla extract

8 cups powdered sugar

7 Tbsp. cocoa

6–8 Tbsp. milk

In the bowl of a stand mixer (or a large mixing bowl) using the paddle attachment, cream butter at medium speed until soft and smooth. Add shortening and extract and beat until combined. Slowly add in powdered sugar and cocoa, beating slightly between each addition. Add milk one tablespoon at a time, beating in between additions until at desired consistency. Turn mixer up to medium-high and beat for 1–2 minutes.

Sweet Swirls

*F*or many bakers, frosting cupcakes is where the challenge begins. My most frequently asked question is "How do you pipe your swirls so nicely?" I won't deny those sweet little swirls do take practice, but I promise that with all the right information and practice, you'll be piping bakery-perfect swirls in no time, and no matter your outcome, your treats will be just as delicious. There are many ways to frost a cupcake. Feel free to experiment with tips and get creative. Below are the steps to get you started piping frosting and a few of my favorite techniques.

PREPARING YOUR PIPING BAG—After your frosting is ready, you'll need to prepare your bag and decide on how you would like your final result to look. No matter what, your taste testers will enjoy their tasty treat!

CHOOSING FROSTING TIPS—Frosting cupcakes starts at the tip! The first thing you'll want to do when frosting is choose your tip. You may choose your tip based on the outcome you would like your cupcakes to have, but you should also consider frosting consistency when choosing a tip. For example, soft frostings don't hold up as well when piped high and may not hold the shape buttercreams can. A soft marshmallow frosting may not hold the shape of a traditional swirl when frosted, but it works perfectly well when piped in a chunky swirl (see Marshmallow-een, page 126) or a small mound (see S'mores, page 122). Recommended tip numbers are included in each technique explanation.

FILLING A PIPING BAG—Place the tip you've chosen down inside the piping bag so the tip is about halfway outside and halfway inside the bag, smaller end outward. Your bag tip may need to be trimmed to fit the tip if new. Remember not to remove too much. You want just enough to allow the tip to protrude halfway out of the bag. Next, gently cup your hand around the piping bag and fold the large open end over your hand. Use a spatula to fill the bag halfway full, pressing the frosting down with the spatula. Filling the bag more than halfway will result in a difficult piping process.

If you're new to piping frosting or sure you'll make a big frosting mess, try following the same steps above with the exception of folding the piping bag over a large glass cup to fill. This will allow better use of your hands, making the process less messy. Be sure to use the spatula to push the frosting down into the small end of the piping bag, leaving less space for air bubbles.

Either way you've filled the bag, once the bag is about halfway full of frosting, pull the open end up again and twist the bag tight where the frosting stops. Some find it easier to use a rubber band or piping bag clip to hold it in place; I like to simply twist the bag so I can easily readjust as I'm piping. Once your piping bag is full and twisted, while holding the piping bag with one hand, use the other to gently work out any air bubbles. Just before piping, squeeze a little bit of frosting back into the bowl to make sure your tip is clear of air.

HOLDING THE PIPING BAG—Once you've made the frosting and brought it to a nice piping consistency, the key to getting those adorable swirls is all in proper holding and pressure, pressure, pressure, and mostly pressure. To properly hold the piping bag, you want to cup your dominant hand around the twist of the bag where the frosting ends. Make sure the bag stays snug between the base of the index finger and thumb resting against your hand. This will help keep the frosting traveling down to the tip of the piping bag and not out the top. You will then use your remaining fingers to apply pressure to the piping bag while using your free hand to guide it.

PIPING—As I said above, it's all about the pressure. Too much pressure will send the frosting quickly out of the bag with little option to control its direction. Too little pressure will make the frosting come out lumpy and will often cause you to drag the frosting. A steady, even pressure will allow you to pipe smooth, even swirls. The key is to pipe frosting with the tip slightly ahead of the frosting, letting it fall into place and releasing pressure just as you complete the swirl. You will need to adjust the amount of pressure depending on the consistency of the frosting. A whipped frosting (see Banana Cream Pie, page 61) will require far less pressure overall than a heavier buttercream frosting.

SWEET SWIRLS

If frosting begins to soften because of your warm hands, place filled piping bag in fridge for a few minutes to chill.

PIPING METHODS—While there are countless tip varieties and frosting types, when it comes to piping cupcake frostings, you always start with the same few techniques of piping, no matter the outcome. You can easily pick how to frost your cupcake by first picking a technique and the tip you'd like to use.

TRADITIONAL SWIRL—This technique will result in the stacked swirl that you traditionally see on cupcakes. Common tips used are open star (Wilton 1M), closed star (Wilton 2D), French star (Ateco 869), large circle (Wilton 2A), and jumbo circle (Ateco 809).

Start by holding the piping bag at a 90-degree angle over the center of the cupcake and apply a small amount of pressure to create a small mound of frosting. (This will help support a tall swirl.) Applying steady pressure, start just inside the 12 o'clock and continue to apply steady pressure while using your non-dominate hand to guide the bag around the mound and back to 12 o'clock, continuing around the mound with less width each time. Just before you reach the top center, slowly release pressure, moving your wrist in a C motion and pulling up to complete the swirl. Do not completely close in the swirl, release pressure, and pull up or you're going to end up with a funky frosting stem on top. (Don't worry if that happens. There are many ways to top your cupcake and hide it!) You can control how short or tall the frosting is by how much you move inward as you pipe each layer. Once you've got a hang of this technique, feel free to skip the mound and instead begin by piping in the center and continue up to the 12 and around. I feel a small mound of frosting in the middle gives beginners a really nice guide and helps stack the frosting.

When using jumbo tips, you can skip the first step of piping a small mound on to the center of the cupcake and start at the center and continue out to the 12 instead. Jumbo circle tips work especially great for soft but fluffy frostings such as marshmallow (see Marshmalloween, page 126).

SWEET SWIRLS

Make this into a rose cupcake by using an open star tip.

CINNAMON ROLL—This technique will result in a flat cupcake frosting with a beautiful design from above. Common tips used are large circle (Wilton 2A) and open star (Wilton 1M).

Holding the tip of the piping bag just above the center of the cupcake at a 90-degree angle, apply even pressure and let the frosting gently fall on the cupcake. Once it has made contact, immediately make a C shape using your guiding hand and continue around in a cinnamon roll–style swirl, letting the frosting fall just behind your tip. Once you approach the edge of the cupcake, gently release pressure while pulling the tip down to a 45-degree angle and away from the cupcake in the same path you were piping the cinnamon roll. If a small "tail" occurs, chill cupcakes for a few minutes and then use a clean paper towel to gently pat the tip in against the frosting.

RUFFLE /MOUND—This is definitely the easiest way to frost a cupcake. This technique will give you a fluffy pile or smooth mound of frosting. Common tips used are open star (Wilton 1M) and jumbo circle (Ateco 809). I often use a jumbo circle tip with this method for frostings that are soft and don't hold up well with other tips.

Hold the tip directly over the center of the cupcake and apply pressure while slowly pulling up. To create a ruffle look using an open star tip (Wilton 1M), you will want to allow the frosting to ruffle out and layer on itself a bit as you slowly pull up with a steady pressure, gently releasing and pulling up when your ruffle is complete. To create a smooth mound of frosting using a jumbo circle tip (Ateco 809), hold the tip over the center of the cupcake, just above the top. Apply a steady pressure, allowing the frosting to flow out toward the sides while you slowly move up, barely above the frosting. Release pressure once the mound is complete.

FLOWER PETAL—Although I call it *flower petal*, the end result can look like much more than flower petals. Cupcakes with multiple mounds of frosting—such as the cupcakes made to look like ice cream (see Ice Cream Sundae, page 58)—are piped the same way. This technique works nicely with thick frostings that "crust" over, like buttercreams. Common tips used are jumbo circle (Ateco 809) and large circle (Wilton 2A).

Hold the piping bag at a 45-degree angle just above the center of the cupcake, pointed out toward the edge of the cupcake. Apply a steady pressure, pushing the frosting toward the edge, and then releasing pressure and pulling the tip away. Continue to do this for as many mounds or petals as you like. If needed, you may chill the cupcakes and smooth any tip with a clean paper towel.

ADDITIONAL FUN EFFECTS—Just when you thought you learned enough about frosting cupcakes, I'm going to throw just a little more cuteness your way! Once you've learned to pipe frosting on cupcakes, you can easily take it one step further by adding a cool effect. You won't believe just how simple it really is.

CREATING TWO-TONED SWIRLS—Adding a second color or even flavor to frosting is really easy and adds major wow factor. To create frosting swirls with two colors of the same frosting, split finished frosting in two and color as needed. Prepare a large piping bag (15-inch works great) with the proper tip and set aside. Fill two uncut, smaller piping bags (12-inch works great) half full of each frosting color, making sure to push the frosting toward the uncut tip to remove air bubbles. Then cut ½ inch off the bottom of the bag (no tip) and slide both bags inside the larger tipped bag you've already prepared. Make sure they are snug down inside the tip and push a little frosting out until both colors are coming out. (I like to

SWEET SWIRLS

A clean paper towel is a helpful tool to have around to smooth out frosting after it has crusted over. It's best to find a paper towel with no indentations on it, such as Viva.

use the beginning frosting to create the little center mounds when possible.) You can do this with three of the same-size bags. Just be sure not to add too much frosting so they won't both fit inside.

SIMPLE STRIPES —Another way to add multiple colors or soft stripes to your piping swirls is to add stripes of gel coloring inside the piping bag. To do this, prepare your piping bag with the proper tip, then fold the bag over your hand (or cup) like normal. But before filling with frosting, use a small food-safe paint brush and paint 3–5 vertical stripes starting down in the tip and continuing all the way up to where the piping bag is folded over. Do this multiple times and with multiple colors if desired, keeping the spacing between the stripes even. Once the coloring stripes are painted, fill with frosting and proceed like normal. This is simple to do; however, you will need to use a different piping bag and paint new stripes each time you fill with frosting. The more stripes you paint, the more color you will add! See an example on Mocha Peppermint Crunch, page 138.

TWO LAYERS—One of my favorite simple ways to decorate a cupcake is by combining two different techniques of piping to create one swirl. To do this, fill two different piping bags using two different tips. Frost one way halfway up and use the other frosting to frost the second half right on top. You can get really creative by using two colors of frosting, two flavors of frosting, or adding a layer of toppings or sprinkles in between. One of the most common two-layer combinations you will see me use is a traditional swirl with a round large tip (Wilton 2A) on bottom and a ruffle on top (Wilton 1M).

Toppers & Toppings

*S*ure, I love baking and frosting cupcakes, but decorating cupcakes is my favorite part. Nothing makes me happier than finishing up a set of cupcakes with the sweetest topper to match. There is a wide variety of ways to decorate a cupcake; your imagination is the limit! Whether you simply add a few sprinkles, mold detailed edible toppers, or purchase premade cupcake toppers, you can find a way to decorate your cupcakes to fit your celebration and time limits.

SPRINKLES—Sprinkles, sprinkles, and more sprinkles! You can't go wrong with sprinkles on a cupcake. It's no secret I'm a sprinkles addict. I can't help it; they're like little specks of happiness. Sprinkles come in many different shapes, sizes, and colors. They are one of the easiest and fastest ways to fancy up a cupcake and they make the perfect addition to any of the options below. A few of the types of sprinkles you will find in this book are jimmies, sanding sugar, holiday mixes, and jumbo shapes. Stores tend to carry the same basic sprinkles all year around, but during almost any holiday you can find new sprinkle mixes in the cake decorating section. You can find just about any type of sprinkle mix possible all year round at online retailers like Amazon, Country Kitchen SweetArt, and Layer Cake Shop. In a pinch, there are a few different tricks you can use to get the colors and combo you want. You can color your own sprinkles by placing white or clear sprinkles in a sandwich bag, adding a small amount of gel coloring and shaking until all of the sprinkles are colored. Another fun way to create your own is to roll out colored fondant and use tiny fondant cutters to cut your own jumbo sprinkles. Leave them out to dry overnight, and then store in a container for up to 6 months.

It's important to note, sprinkles are best added to cupcakes just after piping the frosting. Sometimes a frosting will crust over quickly and the sprinkles will not stick. To prevent this, I pipe and sprinkle only six cupcakes at a time.

CANDY AND EDIBLE TOPPERS—There are all sorts of edible options to top your cupcakes from the candy aisle. Candy is ready to use and available in practically any shape or flavor. It makes a really great option for keeping things sweet and simple. More detailed edible toppers can be bought or made. Recently, more and more premade edible cupcake toppers have been popping up in stores, especially around the holidays. You can often find them in the cake-decorating or holiday baking section. Cake-decorating stores normally carry tons of little edible decorations as well. My favorite place to get these is Country Kitchen SweetArt, which offers a huge selection online. The other edible toppers that I use all the time are DIY fondant toppers. Fondant can be purchased in just about any cake section now and even comes pre-colored for easy use. They can range from a simple shape to an extravagant little sculpted figure. I've kept all fondant toppers in this book simple

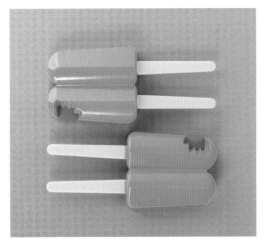

to replicate, with just one color and cut. If you've never used fondant before, it can be as simple as rolling out, cutting, and drying! Leave your toppers to dry on wax paper overnight before placing on top of cupcakes. Do not place in the fridge or they will get soggy. Most edible toppers are best if left off the cupcakes until just before serving. The moisture in the frosting can cause them to get soggy, sticky, or transfer color.

TOPPER TIPS

A fun way to add sprinkles to a cupcake is to rim just the bottom. Place sprinkles in a shallow bowl and roll chilled cupcakes on their side, only allowing the bottom edge to touch the sprinkles.

PLASTIC AND PAPER TOPPERS—Paper and plastic toppers are another great option for giving you a specific theme with little work. Plastic toppers can range from fun little rings to tiny footballs. If it's food-safe, it works! Cake-decorating stores often have hundreds of tiny themed plastic toppers. Paper cupcake toppers have become really popular in the last few years. You can find them in stores, but they are readily available and often free online. Just print, cut, and attach to a lollipop stick. I really love to dress up my paper toppers with straws for a finished look. Plastic toppers can be placed on just after piping and stay on during storage. Paper toppers will need to wait until just before serving.

TOPPINGS—Sometimes you want to skip all the themed cuteness and go straight for the flavor. The ice cream section is a great place to start when looking for premade flavored toppings. Syrups, caramels, preserves, fruits, pie fillings, nuts, cookies—your grocery store is full of delicious foods that will pair perfectly with a cupcake. Most toppings can be placed on right after frosting, but I recommend waiting to apply crunchy and moisture-sensitive toppings until just before severing to prevent them from getting soggy.

CHOCOLATE-COATED—If you're looking for a really fun way to top your cupcakes, why not try dipping them in chocolate? To cover your cupcakes in chocolate, first chill frosted cupcakes in the fridge for 15 minutes. Then fully melt melting chocolate or candy coating in a deep dish using any melting method you prefer until it's nice and smooth. (You may need to add a little shortening to the chocolate to make it smooth.) Make sure you melt enough so that the chocolate is deeper than the height of the cupcake frosting. I like to use a chocolate melter so my chocolate remains the same temperature while I work. To cover the cupcake, simply turn the chilled cupcake upside down, dip it straight in the chocolate, and then pull up. Gently tap any excess chocolate off and turn back right side up to let the chocolate get firm again. I know what you're thinking: You want me to turn my cupcake upside down and dip it in hot chocolate? Don't worry, it's actually much simpler than it sounds, and totally worth the effort!

Tied with a Bow

*Y*ou've just finished baking and decorating your cupcakes and you can't wait to share, but it's not quite time for the party. Or maybe you'd like to share some as a special gift. What now? Let's face it, cupcakes are delicate and need to be properly stored, and packaging them can be even more of a challenge. Below, I'll share information on how to store, transport, package as gifts, and even freeze these treats.

STORING—Most cupcakes are best stored in an airtight container in the fridge; it will keep them moist and extend their freshness by a few days. You can store cupcakes without dairy-heavy frostings or fillings on the counter in an airtight container. Buttercreams that contain small amounts of milk for consistency are safe to leave out on the counter. If your frostings or filling include items that need to be refrigerated—such as cream cheese, whipped topping, pudding, or fruit—you will need to place them in a container in the fridge. I like to use long plastic containers made for cakes and cupcakes to store in my fridge. If you have chosen to use a cardboard bakery box, it's best to wrap the entire box in plastic wrap to keep the cupcakes from going stale or absorbing other odors, but it's not required. I personally keep all of my cupcakes in the fridge, if possible. There are a few exceptions with frostings that will harden too much, such as White Chocolate Raspberry, as noted in the recipe on page 94. Most cupcakes will firm once chilled, so remember to pull them out with enough time to soften up before serving, and place a topper on if needed.

FREEZING—Unfrosted cupcakes freeze well, so if you would like to bake them in advance or store extra to use at a later date, here's an easy way to do so. Simply lay out a large piece of plastic wrap and line up six cupcakes in two rows of three. Wrap them in the plastic wrap and place them in a plastic storage bag or an additional layer of foil to store for 1–2 months. You can also wrap each cupcake individually to use as single-serve treats later on. To thaw cupcakes, remove them from freezer, take off the outside wrap, and leave them on your counter for an hour before unwrapping plastic wrap. Extra condensation will cling to the plastic wrap instead of remaining in the cupcake.

CLAMSHELL CONTAINERS—Clear plastic clamshell cupcake containers like you see at grocery stores are my favorite way to store, transport, and even gift a set of cupcakes. I like using them because they can store and transport cupcakes safely while providing a see-through showcase for my little creations and a blank canvas to decorate! Not only are they functional, but they are inexpensive and convenient. Go ahead and send those cupcakes off to school; no need to return the tray! You can find clamshell containers for cheap at local cake-decorating stores, online, or even local bakeries. Just ask; they will often sell them to you alone! Don't forget that you can always recycle clamshell containers as well.

REUSABLE CONTAINERS—Reusable baked good containers can be nice to have around if you make a lot of baked goods. However, in normal flat-bottom containers, cupcakes can slide around and create buttercream nightmares during transportation. I recommend finding one that has cavities to hold cupcakes in place. When I purchase reusable containers, I look for ones that not only have cupcake cavities and hold 24 cupcakes, but also flip over to a flat surface that can be used with other desserts. These are really handy to have, but they can be pricey. I can buy about 20 disposable clamshell containers for the price of one reusable container. Sometimes you can even find cupcake containers with cavities at dollar stores. I always keep an eye out when visiting.

INDIVIDUAL PACKAGING—What better gift than a sweet individual cupcake wrapped up to go? Individual cupcakes make for really great, inexpensive gifts for teachers, coworkers, and friends. They are the perfect way to say thank you or happy birthday. There are several options available when it comes to individual packaging, including single clamshells, single bakery boxes, or even reusable single cupcake containers. If you're looking for a simple way to package single cupcakes in bulk, you can purchase a pack of clear punch cups and cellophane bags for just a few dollars and place the cupcake inside the cup, then the cup inside the bag, and tie it shut. This is a great bake sale option, and if the cupcake is a little messy, I even include a plastic spoon tied to the outside.

BAKERY BOXES—Though they provide an awesome white canvas to decorate as a gift, bakery boxes are my least favorite option for packaging small groups of cupcakes. Their flexibility can be disastrous with cupcakes, and unless stored right away they allow desserts to dry out quickly. In order to keep them safe, you will need to purchase bakery boxes meant for cupcakes, which come with inserts, or purchase separately. I find that they still tend to have room for disaster as they don't keep the cupcakes snug and can absorb moisture from the cupcake. They can, however, be a good, affordable way to transport large quantities of cupcakes. When I'm transporting a large amount of cupcakes, like for a wedding, I will normally go to my local craft or cake store and buy several full-sheet cake boxes, along with coordinating full-sheet cardboard bottoms (to make the bottom sturdy and less flexible to set the cupcakes on). I will then carefully line up to 48 cupcakes in the box and transport carefully!

BAKER'S TIP

When transporting or serving cupcakes in a warm temperature, store them in the fridge (unless noted otherwise) for several hours to firm beforehand, pulling them out just before transporting to keep them from melting.

RECYCLED CONTAINERS—I am always keeping my eye out for small containers I can reuse to gift baked goods. When you start to pay attention, you will be surprised at the perfect containers that come your way! For example, pretzel shops often use the perfect little doomed containers with pretzel bites. Even egg cartons make the perfect mini cupcake holders. Maybe a friend brought store-bought muffins to the office; the leftover container will make great cupcake packaging later on. Just a quick wash and you're good to go. Instead of consuming one too many cupcakes, next time you can grab a container from your stash and send the extras to the office, school, church, or wherever—cupcakes are always welcome!

DECORATIONS—Adorable cupcakes are such a fun gift to give, but a little decorating pizzazz is the cherry on top! Baker's twine, printable tags, patterned paper, paper shred, and bows are my favorite things to add to a package of cupcakes. Small trinkets can also be fun to add, like bells at Christmastime or a candle on a birthday. For a special birthday, why not make it a party? Along with a special birthday cupcake, include a balloon, sprinkles, and a candle.

TAGS & CARDS—If you're super awesome, you may already have a stash of handmade thank you cards on hand. But if you're anything like me, you're going to need another option! With a quick online search, you can find hundreds of printable tags to top your sweet gift and get the message across. Bloggers all around the world offer up their printable creations for you to use. Just print, cut, and use. When I find a great tag or card, I like to print out extra and keep them in a small container for a really quick gift with little effort. Tags also make a great place to write down flavors or ingredient information. For example, you may want to write "Mocha Swirl Cupcakes" on back or warn that the cupcakes contain nuts. Tags can be useful and adorable.

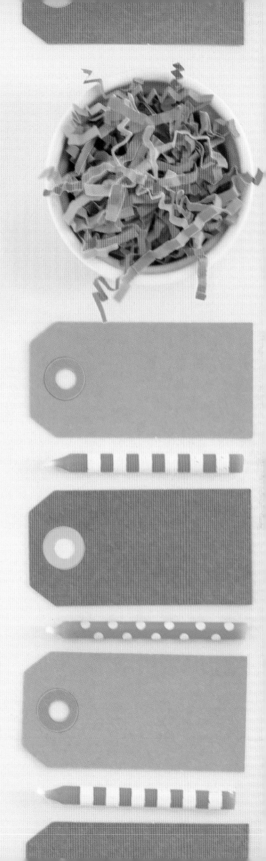

Before You Bake

Wait, hold the spatula! Before you preheat that oven, I have a few more tricks, tips, and information bits to help make your party-perfect cupcake experience a little more magical!

BAKING

Wrong Temperatures—Ovens can be a bit deceptive. To help ensure your baked goods are going to come out properly, it's a good idea to purchase an oven thermometer and double check the temperature occasionally, especially if you have reoccurring baking complications.

Fallen Cake—Cupcakes will naturally fall a bit after removing them from the oven. If your cupcakes have fallen a great deal and sunk, chances are you've overmixed the batter, causing too many air bubbles and not enough stable cake. Gummy cupcake tops are also a sign of poorly mixed cake batter as well.

Muffin Tops—Sometimes cake batter can bake up and over the liners onto the pan, making it pretty hard to remove and messy looking. Normally, the culprit of cupcake muffin tops is simply adding too much batter. If you weren't measuring out your batter before, try measuring out exactly 3 level tablespoons.

Peeling Liners—Sometimes cupcake liners will peel away from the edge when stored. This is often the sign of a poor quality liner. If this has already occurred, one trick you can use is to place an unbaked cupcake liner around the outside of the peeling cupcake liner to give it a two-layer look.

Short Cakes—Make sure your oven is completely preheated before placing cupcakes in to bake. Rising agents within the cake mix will not react until a particular temperature is reached, causing flat, small cupcakes. It's also important to check the use-by date on your cake mix; cake mixes past this date may not rise properly.

Air Bubbles on Cupcakes—If you have little "bubbles" baking on top of your cupcakes, you probably have too many large

SPRINKLES OF THOUGHT

While baking your way through Cupcakery, you'll notice these special highlighted sections with ways to make your cupcakes even better.

MIX IT UP
Keep your options open with these recipe additions.

PARTY-PERFECT
Decorating or styling tips that will easily help make your cupcakes the center of the party.

BAKER'S TIPS
Tips to make your baking adventure a sweet success in the kitchen.

SWEET SWIRLS
Tips and information on how to achieve the cupcake frosting as shown, or an additional twist.

TOPPER TIPS
Additional topper or decorating ideas to add the finishing touches to your cupcakes.

air bubbles in your batter. One helpful trick you can try is to firmly tap your cupcake pan on the counter 2–3 times before baking. This will help pop the excess air bubbles that may be trapped.

Cake Mix Clumps—If you're finding that there are noticeable clumps of cake mix in your cake batter and you've already sifted your dry ingredients, the culprit is most likely ingredient temperatures. If you've used a very cold liquid it may cause your cake mix to curd together. Try letting your liquid come to a room temperature. This is especially true with cupcakes that contain soda as a liquid, such as Grape Soda (page 50) or Cherry Cola (page 53).

• •

FROSTING

Clogged Frosting Tip—If you are trying to frost cupcakes with a star tip and the frosting keeps clogging in the tip, you have one of two problems: lumps from underbeating the butter and shortening or lumps of powdered sugar. Even if you can wiggle the lump out of the tip, it's a safe bet that if there's one, there's more. Pipe all of your frosting back into your bowl and rewhip the frosting until smooth. Run a spatula along the frosting and smooth it back and forth to try and see if any more lumps are in there.

Frosting Air Pockets—Air pockets in your piping bag will certainly wreak havoc on your piping job. And unfortunately you won't know it until it happens. To help minimize air pockets, make sure to press frosting all the way down into the tip when filling the bag. After it's full, massage the frosting down to the tip before twisting, and then squeeze a bit back into the bowl before piping.

Frosting Consistency—Frosting should easily flow from the piping tip. If you are applying a lot of pressure and your frosting is coming out clumpy, your frosting is probably too thick. Pipe the frosting back in the bowl and add a little more liquid and rewhip. If you find your frosting is too soft and unstable, you can pipe the frosting back in the bowl and add more powdered sugar a few tablespoons at a time, whipping in between each addition.

Grainy Frosting—Sometimes frosting can have a bit of a gritty feel to it. Often I find this problem resolves itself after the frosting has had time to sit, allowing the powdered sugar to absorb more of the moisture. If you continue to find this is a problem, make sure you're using a quality-brand powdered sugar. If this still remains a problem, try putting the powdered sugar in a food processor before using to make it even finer.

Achieving Bold Frosting Colors—Some bold or dark frosting colors such as red or black can be hard to achieve. The problem with these colors is that they often take so much coloring that the frosting consistency changes, often making the frosting less smooth and too soft for nice piping. Truthfully, I try to avoid making dark-colored frosting, but if needed, it's best to start with a good quality gel coloring, like Ameri-Color. Make sure to add in the gel coloring before adding in the liquid to give yourself a little more control over the consistency. Remember the frosting color will deepen by at least one shade after sitting overnight. Another trick you can try to obtain a dark frosting color without the hassle is to use an edible coloring spray, often found in the cake-decorating section of craft stores.

Sinking/Melting Frosting—If your frosting is sinking or melting after being piped, there are a few things you should check. First, make sure your cupcakes are completely cool all the way through before frosting. It's possible that the cupcake tops are cool but there's still a bit of heat left in the middle, which eventually will escape right into your frosting, causing it to melt. It's important to let the cupcakes cool for 20 to 30 minutes after pulling them from the oven. If you're in a hurry, you can place the cupcakes in the fridge for a few minutes to help speed up the process. If you're sure the cupcakes were cool yet the frosting still sunk or begun to melt, I would assume the problem is over-moistened frosting. If it's not too late, you can place the frosting back in the bowl and add a little powdered sugar to it to bring it to a thicker consistency. Also, be sure to move the frosted cupcakes away from the oven and baking pans. Even cooling down, the oven can still give off heat, which may melt the frosting.

DECORATING

Sliding Sprinkles—When adding sprinkles to cupcakes, pipe cupcakes no more than six at a time and pause to decorate those cupcakes. Most frostings will begin to crust over after a few moments, causing sprinkles to roll right off. This is more of a problem when using round tips that don't create crevices for the sprinkles to rest.

Toppers Cracking Frosting—If possible, add any sprinkles and toppers right after frosting. If you wait for a while, your frosting may crust and crack once a topper is placed on it. The same goes for cold frosting. If you need to add your toppers later (fondant or paper) and your cupcakes have been in the fridge, let them come to room temperature before gently placing the toppers on.

Everyday Occasions

Blueberry-Stuffed French Toast

Dessert for breakfast? I'm in! If the sweet swirl of maple buttercream isn't enough to win you over, the fruit filling surprise will be sure to do the trick!

MAKES 24–30 CUPCAKES

FRENCH TOAST CUPCAKES

1 box yellow cake mix

1 tsp. cinnamon + additional for sprinkling

⅛ tsp. nutmeg

4 large eggs

½ cup sour cream

1 cup milk

¼ cup melted butter (slightly cooled)

FILLING

1 small can of blueberry pie filling

MAPLE BUTTERCREAM

2 cups unsalted butter

1 Tbsp. maple extract (McCormick)

8 cups powdered sugar

6–8 Tbsp. milk

powdered sugar to top

MIX IT UP

Create even more fun flavors by swapping out the filling for other pie fillings.

1. Preheat oven to 350 degrees. Line two 12-cup cupcake pans with cupcake liners and set aside.

2. In a medium mixing bowl, sift together cake mix, cinnamon, and nutmeg and set aside. In the bowl of a stand mixer (or large mixing bowl) using the paddle attachment, beat together eggs, sour cream, and milk at a low speed. Add dry ingredients and beat until just combined. Beat in melted butter until just combined. Once all ingredients are incorporated, scrape the sides and bottom of the bowl and turn mixer up to medium and beat once more for 15–20 seconds. Do not overbeat.

3. Spoon three tablespoons of batter into each cupcake liner and sprinkle a little cinnamon on top. Bake on middle oven rack for 16–18 minutes, baking up to 24 cupcakes side by side at a time. (For best results, bake cupcakes one pan at a time.) Once a toothpick comes out clean, remove from oven and allow cupcakes to rest in pan for 2–4 minutes before removing and transferring to a cooling rack. Prepare pan and repeat this step with any remaining batter.

4. While cupcakes are cooling, prepare frosting. In the bowl of a stand mixer (or large mixing bowl) using the paddle attachment, cream butter at medium speed until soft and smooth. Add maple extract and beat until combined. Slowly add in powdered sugar, beating slightly between each addition. Add milk one tablespoon at a time, beating in between additions until at desired consistency. Turn mixer up to medium-high and beat for 1–2 minutes.

5. Once cupcakes have completely cooled, core and fill cupcakes with fruit filling. Pipe maple buttercream on cupcakes using the traditional swirl technique (page 24) with a large circle tip. Store in the refrigerator and dust with powdered sugar just before serving.

Cinnamon Roll

If only cinnamon rolls were as easy to make as they are to enjoy.
These cupcakes are half the work but all the yummy!

MAKES 24–30 CUPCAKES

CINNAMON CUPCAKES

1 box yellow cake mix

4 Tbsp. instant vanilla pudding

1 Tbsp. sugar

1½ Tbsp. cinnamon

4 large eggs

½ cup sour cream

1 cup milk

¼ cup melted butter (slightly cooled)

CREAM CHEESE CINNAMON FROSTING

1 cup unsalted butter

1 (8-oz.) pkg. cream cheese

1 tsp. vanilla extract

1 packet Duncan Hines Cinnamon Roll Frosting Creations

6 cups powdered sugar

4–6 Tbsp. milk

MIX IT UP

For a special treat, enjoy these cinnamon roll cupcakes warmed up in the microwave for a few seconds.

1. Preheat oven to 350 degrees. Line two 12-cup cupcake pans with cupcake liners and set aside.

2. In a medium mixing bowl, sift together cake mix and pudding and set aside. In a small bowl, mix cinnamon and sugar and set aside. In the bowl of a stand mixer (or large mixing bowl) using the paddle attachment, beat together eggs, sour cream, and milk at low speed. Add the cake and pudding mix and beat until just combined. Beat in melted butter until just combined. Once all ingredients are incorporated, scrape the sides and bottom of the bowl and turn mixer up to medium and beat once more for 15–20 seconds. Do not overbeat.

3. Spoon three tablespoons of batter and ¼ teaspoon cinnamon sugar into each cupcake liner, alternating batter and cinnamon sugar. Sprinkle any remaining cinnamon sugar on the top of the cupcake batter and give each set of cupcake batter a swirl with a toothpick. Bake on middle oven rack for 16–18 minutes, baking up to 24 cupcakes side by side at a time. (For best results, bake cupcakes one pan at a time.) Once a toothpick comes out clean, remove from oven and allow cupcakes to rest in pan for 2–4 minutes before removing and transferring to a cooling rack. Prepare pan and repeat this step with any remaining batter.

4. While cupcakes are cooling, prepare frosting. In the bowl of a stand mixer (or large mixing bowl) using the paddle attachment, cream butter at medium speed until soft and smooth. Add cream cheese, vanilla extract, and Frosting Creation and beat until combined. Slowly add in powdered sugar, beating slightly between each addition. Add milk one tablespoon at a time, beating in between additions until at desired consistency. Turn mixer up to medium-high and beat for 1–2 minutes.

5. Once cupcakes have completely cooled, pipe cream cheese cinnamon frosting onto cupcakes using the cinnamon roll technique (page 25) with a large circle tip. Store in an airtight container in the fridge until served.

Mocha Swirl

Chocolate and coffee are possibly two of the world's greatest flavors separately, but when you mix the two, sweet magic happens! Coffee and chocolate lovers can have it all with this combo.

MAKES 24–30 CUPCAKES

MOCHA CUPCAKES

1 box chocolate fudge cake mix

4 large eggs

½ cup sour cream

1 cup + 3 Tbsp. coffee (slightly cooled)

1 Tbsp. coffee extract

¼ cup melted butter (slightly cooled)

MOCHA BUTTERCREAM

1 cup unsalted butter

1 cup shortening

2 Tbsp. coffee extract

5 Tbsp. cocoa powder

8 cups powdered sugar

5–7 Tbsp. milk

24–30 coffee beans to top

PARTY-PERFECT

This combo would make the perfect cupcake for an adult get-together. Ladies' night, coffee and cupcakes, or game night—it's the perfect treat!

1. Preheat oven to 350 degrees. Line two 12-cup cupcake pans with cupcake liners and set aside.

2. In a medium mixing bowl, sift cake mix and set aside. In the bowl of a stand mixer (or large mixing bowl) using the paddle attachment, beat together eggs, sour cream, coffee, and coffee extract at low speed. Add the cake mix and beat until just combined. Beat in melted butter until just combined. Once all ingredients are incorporated, scrape the sides and bottom of the bowl and turn mixer up to medium and beat once more for 15–20 seconds. Do not overbeat.

3. Spoon three tablespoons of batter into each cupcake liner and bake on middle oven rack for 18–20 minutes, baking up to 24 cupcakes side by side at a time. (For best results bake cupcakes one pan at a time.) Once a toothpick comes out clean, remove from oven and allow cupcakes to rest in pan for 2–4 minutes before removing and transferring to a cooling rack. Prepare pan and repeat this step with any remaining batter.

4. While cupcakes are cooling, prepare buttercream. In the bowl of a stand mixer (or large mixing bowl) using the paddle attachment, cream butter at medium speed until soft and smooth. Add shortening and coffee extract and beat until combined. Slowly add in powdered sugar and cocoa, beating slightly between each addition. Add milk one tablespoon at a time, beating in between additions until at desired consistency. Turn mixer up to medium-high and beat for 1–2 minutes.

5. Once cupcakes have completely cooled, pipe mocha buttercream on cupcakes using the traditional swirl technique (page 24) with a large circle tip. Top with coffee beans, chocolate-covered coffee beans, or chocolate sprinkles if desired.

Tutti Frutti

It's no secret cereal is much more than breakfast; it also makes the perfect lunch, snack, and dinner. Now you can have your dessert and eat your cereal too—no spoon required.

MAKES 24–30 CUPCAKES

VANILLA CUPCAKES

1 box white cake mix

4 Tbsp. instant vanilla pudding

4 large egg whites

½ cup sour cream

1¼ cup milk

¼ cup melted butter (slightly cooled)

1 cup crushed fruit ring cereal

FRUTTI BUTTERCREAM

1 cup butter

1 cup shortening

1 dram tutti frutti candy flavoring

1½ tsp. lemon extract

8 cups powdered sugar

6–8 Tbsp. milk

TOPPING

fruit ring cereal

MIX IT UP

Have a little fun trying different fruit cereals in the recipe, or have a lot of fun and mix in a few different types.

1. Preheat oven to 350 degrees. Line two 12-cup cupcake pans with cupcake liners and set aside.

2. In a medium mixing bowl, sift together cake mix and pudding and set aside. In the bowl of a stand mixer (or large mixing bowl) using the paddle attachment, beat together egg whites, sour cream, and milk at low speed. Add dry ingredients and beat until just combined. Beat in melted butter until just combined. Once all ingredients are incorporated, scrape the sides and bottom of the bowl and turn mixer up to medium and beat once more for 15–20 seconds. Do not overbeat. Fold in crushed fruit cereal.

3. Spoon three tablespoons of batter into each cupcake liner and bake on middle oven rack for 16–18 minutes, baking up to 24 cupcakes side by side at a time. (For best results, bake cupcakes one pan at a time.) Once a toothpick comes out clean, remove from oven and allow cupcakes to rest in pan for 2–4 minutes before removing and transferring to a cooling rack. Prepare pan and repeat this step with any remaining batter.

4. While cupcakes are cooling, prepare frosting. In the bowl of a stand mixer (or large mixing bowl) using the paddle attachment, cream butter at medium speed until soft and smooth. Add shortening, candy flavoring, and lemon extract and beat until combined. Slowly add in powdered sugar, beating slightly between each addition. Add milk one tablespoon at a time, beating in between additions until at desired consistency. Turn mixer up to medium-high and beat for 1–2 minutes.

5. Once cupcakes have completely cooled, pipe tutti frutti buttercream on cupcakes using the traditional swirl technique (page 24) and a jumbo circle tip. Top with fruit cereal just before serving.

Grape Soda

Grape is one of those flavors you just never outgrow. Kids and adults alike will love these grape soda-inspired treats. Grab a straw and a soda; it's about to get bubbly!

MAKES 24–30 CUPCAKES

GRAPE CUPCAKES

1 box white cake mix

¼ cup flour

3 large eggs

12 oz. grape soda (room temperature)

purple gel coloring

GRAPE SODA FROSTING

1 cup unsalted butter

1 cup shortening

1 packet grape Kool-Aid

6–8 Tbsp. grape soda

purple gel coloring

PARTY-PERFECT

For a bubbly grape display, serve cupcakes on a tray surrounded by small and large grape gumballs.

1. Preheat oven to 350 degrees. Line two 12-cup cupcake pans with cupcake liners and set aside.

2. In a medium mixing bowl, sift together cake mix and flour and set aside. In the bowl of a stand mixer (or large mixing bowl) using the paddle attachment, beat together eggs and grape soda at low speed. Add the dry ingredients and a small amount of purple coloring. Beat until just combined. Once all ingredients are incorporated, scrape the sides and bottom of the bowl and turn mixer up to medium and beat once more for 15–20 seconds. Do not overbeat.

3. Spoon three tablespoons of batter into each cupcake liner and bake on middle oven rack for 16–18 minutes, baking up to 24 cupcakes side by side at a time. (For best results, bake cupcakes one pan at a time.) Once a toothpick comes out clean, remove from oven and allow cupcakes to rest in pan for 2–4 minutes before removing and transferring to a cooling rack. Prepare pan and repeat this step with any remaining batter.

4. While cupcakes are cooling, prepare frosting. In the bowl of a stand mixer (or large mixing bowl) using the paddle attachment, cream butter at medium speed until soft and smooth. Add shortening and Kool-Aid and beat until combined. Slowly add in powdered sugar, beating slightly between each addition. Add small amounts of purple coloring and grape soda one tablespoon at a time, beating in between additions until at desired consistency and color. Turn mixer up to medium-high and beat for 1–2 minutes.

5. Once cupcakes have completely cooled, frost cupcakes with grape soda buttercream using the traditional swirl technique (page 24) and a large circle tip.

Cherry Cola

These cherry cola cupcakes bring a whole new meaning to "pretty please with a cherry on top." You'll have cherry cola fans begging for more with these little sweeties.

MAKES 24–30 CUPCAKES

CHOCOLATE CHERRY CUPCAKES

1 box chocolate cake mix

¼ cup flour

3 large eggs

½ cup sour cream

12 oz. cherry cola (room temperature)

CHERRY COLA BUTTERCREAM

1 cup unsalted butter

1 cup shortening

1 tsp. cherry extract

¼ tsp. cola flavoring

8 cups powdered sugar

6–8 Tbsp. cherry cola

TOPPINGS

24–30 cherries

chocolate sprinkles

TOPPER TIPS

Create unique toppers by gluing recycled metal cola lids to lollipop sticks. Add paper backing or hanging twine for even more pizzazz.

1. Preheat oven to 350 degrees. Line two 12-cup cupcake pans with cupcake liners and set aside.

2. In a medium mixing bowl, sift cake and flour and set aside. In the bowl of a stand mixer (or large mixing bowl) using the paddle attachment, beat together eggs, sour cream, and cherry cola at low speed. Add dry ingredients and beat until just combined. Once all ingredients are incorporated, scrape the sides and bottom of the bowl and turn mixer up to medium and beat once more for 15–20 seconds. Do not overbeat.

3. Spoon three tablespoons of batter into each cupcake liner and bake on middle oven rack for 16–18 minutes, baking up to 24 cupcakes side by side at a time. (For best results, bake cupcakes one pan at a time.) Once a toothpick comes out clean, remove from oven and allow cupcakes to rest in pan for 2–4 minutes before removing and transferring to a cooling rack. Prepare pan and repeat this step with any remaining batter.

4. While cupcakes are cooling, prepare frosting. In the bowl of a stand mixer (or large mixing bowl) using the paddle attachment, cream butter at medium speed until soft and smooth. Add shortening, cherry extract, and cola flavoring and beat until combined. Slowly add in powdered sugar, beating slightly between each addition. Add cherry cola one tablespoon at a time, beating in between additions until at desired consistency. Turn mixer up to medium-high and beat for 1–2 minutes.

5. Once cupcakes have completely cooled, frost cupcakes with cherry cola buttercream using the traditional swirl technique (page 24) and an open star tip. Top with cherries and chocolate sprinkles if desired.

Root Beer Float

MAKES 24–30 CUPCAKES

ROOT BEER CUPCAKES

1 box white cake mix

¼ cup flour

3 large eggs

12 oz. root beer (room temperature)

1 Tbsp. root beer concentrate

ROOT BEER BUTTERCREAM

½ cup unsalted butter

½ cup shortening

2 Tbsp. root beer concentrate

4 cups powdered sugar

2–3 Tbsp. milk

brown gel coloring

VANILLA BUTTERCREAM

½ cup unsalted butter

½ cup shortening

1 Tbsp. vanilla extract

4 cups powdered sugar

3–4 Tbsp. milk

SWEET SWIRLS

Create a true root beer float look! Pipe a swirl of root beer buttercream with the cinnamon roll technique and then add a scoop of vanilla buttercream like ice cream.

1. Preheat oven to 350 degrees. Line two 12-cup cupcake pans with cupcake liners and set aside.

2. In a medium mixing bowl, sift cake mix and flour and set aside. Beat together eggs, root beer, and root beer concentrate at low speed. Add cake mix and beat until just combined. Once all ingredients are incorporated, scrape the sides and bottom of the bowl and turn mixer up to medium and beat once more for 15–20 seconds. Do not overbeat.

3. Spoon three tablespoons of batter into each cupcake liner and bake on middle oven rack for 16–18 minutes, baking up to 24 cupcakes side by side at a time. (For best results, bake cupcakes one pan at a time.) Once a toothpick comes out clean, remove from oven and allow cupcakes to rest in pan for 2–4 minutes before removing and transferring to a cooling rack. Prepare pan and repeat this step with any remaining batter.

4. While cupcakes are cooling, prepare frostings. To prepare root beer buttercream, cream butter at medium speed until soft and smooth. Add shortening and root beer concentrate and beat until combined. Slowly add in powdered sugar, beating slightly between each addition. Add small amounts of brown gel coloring and milk one tablespoon at a time, beating in between additions until desired consistency and color is achieved. Turn mixer up to medium-high and beat for 1–2 minutes.

5. For vanilla buttercream, in the bowl of a stand mixer (or large mixing bowl) using the paddle attachment, cream butter at medium speed until soft and smooth. Add shortening and vanilla extract and beat until combined. Slowly add in powdered sugar, beating slightly between each addition. Add milk one tablespoon at a time, beating in between additions until at desired consistency. Turn mixer up to medium-high and beat for 1–2 minutes.

6. Once cupcakes have completely cooled, frost cupcakes with the traditional swirl technique (page 24) combined with the two-toned effect (page 26) using a large circle tip.

Chocolate Malt

MAKES 24–30 CUPCAKES

CHOCOLATE CUPCAKES

1 box chocolate cake mix

4 Tbsp. instant chocolate pudding

4 large eggs

½ cup sour cream

1 cup milk

¼ cup melted butter (slightly cooled)

CHOCOLATE MALT BUTTERCREAM

1 cup chocolate malt powder

1 cup unsalted butter

1 cup shortening

1 tsp. vanilla extract

8 cups powdered sugar

6–8 Tbsp. milk

TOPPINGS

2 cups heavy whipping cream

4 Tbsp. powdered sugar

24–30 cherries

PARTY-PERFECT

For a fun retro "twist," serve these cupcakes on old records used as platters.

1. Preheat oven to 350 degrees. Line two 12-cup cupcake pans with cupcake liners and set aside.

2. In a medium mixing bowl, sift together cake mix and pudding and set aside. In the bowl of a stand mixer (or large mixing bowl) using the paddle attachment, beat together eggs, sour cream, and milk at low speed. Add dry ingredients and beat until just combined. Beat in melted butter until just combined. Once all ingredients are incorporated, scrape the sides and bottom of the bowl and turn mixer up to medium and beat once more for 15–20 seconds. Do not overbeat.

3. Spoon three tablespoons of batter into each cupcake liner and bake on middle oven rack for 16–18 minutes, baking up to 24 cupcakes side by side at a time. (For best results, bake cupcakes one pan at a time.) Once a toothpick comes out clean, remove from oven and allow cupcakes to rest in pan for 2–4 minutes before removing and transferring to a cooling rack. Prepare pan and repeat this step with any remaining batter.

4. While cupcakes are cooling, prepare frosting and topping. In a small bowl, combine chocolate malt powder and four tablespoons of milk and set aside. In the bowl of a stand mixer (or large mixing bowl) using the paddle attachment, cream butter at medium speed until soft and smooth. Add shortening and vanilla extract and beat until combined. Slowly add in powdered sugar, beating slightly between each addition. Pour in dissolved chocolate malt and beat until combined. Add milk one tablespoon at a time, beating in between additions until at desired consistency. Turn mixer up to medium-high and beat for 1–2 minutes.

5. To prepare whipped topping, chill a large metal mixing bowl and whisk attachment. Once cold, beat heavy whipping cream on medium-high until stiff peaks have formed. Beat in powdered sugar.

6. Once cupcakes have completely cooled, pipe chocolate malt buttercream and whipping cream using the two-layer effect. Keep refrigerated, and top with cherries just before serving.

Ice Cream Sundae

I scream, you scream, we all scream for ice cream … cupcakes! Give them something to really cheer about with these fun cupcakes made to look just like a classic ice cream sundae. Go ahead, have three scoops and sprinkles on top.

MAKES 24–30 CUPCAKES

CHOCOLATE FUDGE CUPCAKES

1 box chocolate fudge cake mix

4 Tbsp. instant chocolate pudding

4 large eggs

½ cup sour cream

1 cup milk

¼ cup melted butter (slightly cooled)

VANILLA BUTTERCREAM

1 cup unsalted butter

1 cup shortening

1 Tbsp. vanilla extract

8 cups powdered sugar

6–8 Tbsp. vanilla coffee creamer

TOPPINGS

6 oz. hot fudge topping

rainbow sprinkles

24–30 candy cherries

TOPPING TIPS

Easily pipe on fudge by first placing the fudge in a decorating bottle.

1. Preheat oven to 350 degrees. Line two 12-cup cupcake pans with cupcake liners and set aside.

2. In a medium mixing bowl, sift together cake mix and pudding and set aside. In the bowl of a stand mixer (or large mixing bowl) using the paddle attachment, beat together eggs, sour cream, and milk at low speed. Add dry ingredients and beat until just combined. Beat in melted butter until just combined. Once all ingredients are incorporated, scrape the sides and bottom of the bowl and turn mixer up to medium and beat once more for 15–20 seconds. Do not overbeat.

3. Spoon three tablespoons of batter into each cupcake liner and bake on middle oven rack for 16–18 minutes, baking up to 24 cupcakes side by side at a time. (For best results, bake cupcakes one pan at a time.) Once a toothpick comes out clean, remove from oven and allow cupcakes to rest in pan for 2–4 minutes before removing and transferring to a cooling rack. Prepare pan and repeat this step with any remaining batter.

4. While cupcakes are cooling, prepare frosting. In the bowl of a stand mixer (or large mixing bowl) using the paddle attachment, cream butter at medium speed until soft and smooth. Add shortening and vanilla extract and beat until combined. Slowly add in powdered sugar, beating slightly between each addition. Add creamer one tablespoon at a time, beating in between additions until at desired consistency. Turn mixer up to medium-high and beat for 1–2 minutes.

5. Once cupcakes have completely cooled, frost cupcakes with vanilla buttercream using the flower petal technique (page 26) and a jumbo circle tip. Once frosted, place in fridge to chill until buttercream firms slightly. Once chilled, use a clean paper towel to quickly smooth out each mount tip. Top with hot fudge, sprinkles, and candy cherries.

Banana Cream Pie

If you're looking for a treat that's light and sweet, these are it!
You won't believe how much these really taste like a banana cream pie.
But watch out, it's hard to stop at just one. You just may go bananas!

MAKES 24–30 CUPCAKES

BANANA CUPAKES

1 box yellow cake mix

4 Tbsp. instant banana cream pudding

4 large eggs

½ sour cream

1 cup milk

¼ cup melted butter (slightly cooled)

BANANA CREAM FILLING

12 Tbsp. instant banana cream pudding

2 cups milk

WHIPPED CREAM TOPPING

2 cups heavy whipping cream

1 tsp. vanilla extract

8 Tbsp. powdered sugar

24 small vanilla wafers to top

¼ cup vanilla wafer crumbs to top

MIX IT UP

Switch out the whipped topping for marshmallow frosting (page 122) for a banana moon pie cupcake!

1. Preheat oven to 350 degrees. Line two 12-cup cupcake pans with cupcake liners and set aside.

2. In medium mixing bowl, sift together cake mix and pudding and set aside. In the bowl of a stand mixer (or large mixing bowl) using the paddle attachment, beat together eggs, sour cream, and milk. Add dry ingredients and beat until just combined. Beat in melted butter until just combined. Once all ingredients are incorporated, make sure to scrape the sides and bottom of the bowl and turn mixer up to medium and beat once more for 15–20 seconds. Do not overbeat.

3. Spoon three tablespoons of batter into each cupcake liner and bake on middle oven rack for 16–18 minutes, baking up to 24 cupcakes side by side at a time. (For best results, bake cupcakes one pan at a time.) Once a toothpick comes out clean, remove from oven and allow cupcakes to rest in pan for 2–4 minutes before removing and transferring to a cooling rack. Prepare pan and repeat this step with any remaining batter.

4. While cupcakes are cooling, prepare filling and whipped topping. To prepare filling, whisk together instant pudding and milk in a small mixing bowl. Place in fridge to chill. To prepare whipped topping, place large metal mixing bowl and electric whisk attachment(s) into freezer to chill. Once cold, remove chilled bowl from freezer and beat heavy whipping cream until stiff peaks have formed. Add in powdered sugar and vanilla extract and beat once more just until combined.

5. Once cupcakes have completely cooled, core cupcakes and fill with banana cream filling. Frost cupcakes with whipped topping using the traditional swirl technique (page 24) and a jumbo circle tip. Top with crushed cookie crumbs and small vanilla wafers. Store in an airtight container and refrigerate until served.

Cherry Cheesecake

MAKES 24–30 CUPCAKES

CHEESECAKE CUPCAKES

1 box white cake mix

4 Tbsp. instant cheesecake pudding

4 large egg whites

½ cup sour cream

1¼ cup milk

¼ cup melted butter (slightly cooled)

CHEESECAKE FROSTING

4 Tbsp. instant cheesecake pudding

1 cup unsalted butter

1 (8-oz.) pkg. cream cheese

1 tsp. vanilla extract

6 cups powdered sugar

4–6 Tbsp. milk

TOPPING

1 small can cherry pie filling

¼ cup graham cracker crumbs

MIX IT UP

Why stop at just cherry cheesecake? Mix things up a bit by topping with your favorite cheesecake mix-ins, from caramel to brownie bits.

1. Preheat oven to 350 degrees. Line two 12-cup cupcake pans with cupcake liners and set aside.

2. In a medium mixing bowl, sift together cake mix and pudding and set aside. Beat together egg whites, sour cream, and milk at low speed. Add dry ingredients and beat until just combined. Beat in melted butter until just combined. Once all ingredients are incorporated, scrape the sides and bottom of the bowl and turn mixer up to medium and beat once more for 15–20 seconds. Do not overbeat.

3. Spoon three tablespoons of batter into each cupcake liner and bake on middle oven rack for 16–18 minutes, baking up to 24 cupcakes side by side at a time. (For best results, bake cupcakes one pan at a time.) Once a toothpick comes out clean, remove from oven and allow cupcakes to rest in pan for 2–4 minutes before removing and transferring to a cooling rack. Prepare pan and repeat this step with any remaining batter.

4. While cupcakes are cooling, prepare frosting. Whisk together instant cheesecake pudding and four tablespoons of milk in a small bowl and set aside. Cream butter at medium speed until soft and smooth. Add cream cheese and vanilla extract and beat until combined. Slowly add in powdered sugar, beating slightly between each addition. Add pudding mix and then add milk one tablespoon at a time, beating in between additions until at desired consistency. Turn mixer up to medium-high and beat for 1–2 minutes.

5. Once cupcakes have completely cooled, frost cupcakes with cheesecake frosting using the traditional swirl technique (page 24) and a large circle tip. Sprinkle tops with graham cracker crumbs and place in fridge for 5 minutes to chill. Then, using the back of a teaspoon, press a small dent into the tops of the frosting and spoon pie filling on top (the dent will help keep topping in place). Store in an airtight container in the fridge until ready to be served.

Monster Cookie Dough

Finally, cookie dough you can eat! A little of this, a little of that,
these monster cookie dough cupcakes live up to their name.
You can have it all, so go ahead and lick the spoon.

MAKES 24–30 CUPCAKES

YELLOW CUPCAKES

1 box yellow cake mix

4 Tbsp. instant vanilla pudding

4 large eggs

½ cup sour cream

1 cup milk

¼ cup melted butter (slightly cooled)

MONSTER COOKIE DOUGH FROSTING

⅓ cup brown sugar

¾ cup flour

6 cups powdered sugar

1½ cup unsalted butter

1½ tsp. vanilla extract

6–8 Tbsp. milk

1 cup quick oats

¾ cup M&Ms

¾ cup mini chocolate chips

PARTY-PERFECT

These cupcakes would make the perfect school-themed cupcakes. Add chocolate letter toppers and you're all set for a back-to-school bash!

1. Preheat oven to 350 degrees. Line two 12-cup cupcake pans with cupcake liners and set aside.

2. In a medium mixing bowl, sift together cake mix and pudding and set aside. In the bowl of a stand mixer (or large mixing bowl) using the paddle attachment, beat together eggs, sour cream, and milk at low speed. Add the dry ingredients and beat until just combined. Beat in melted butter until just combined. Once all ingredients are incorporated, scrape the sides and bottom of the bowl and turn mixer up to medium-high and beat once more for 30 seconds.

3. Spoon three tablespoons of batter into each cupcake liner and bake on middle oven rack for 16–18 minutes, baking up to 24 cupcakes side by side at a time. (For best results, bake cupcakes one pan at a time.) Once a toothpick comes out clean, remove from oven and allow cupcakes to rest in pan for 2–4 minutes before removing and transferring to a cooling rack. Prepare pan and repeat this step with any remaining batter.

4. While cupcakes are cooling, prepare frosting. In a large mixing bowl, whisk together brown sugar, flour, and powdered sugar and set aside. In the bowl of a stand mixer (or large mixing bowl) using the paddle attachment, cream butter at medium speed until soft and smooth. Add vanilla extract and beat until combined. Slowly add in dry ingredients, beating slightly between each addition. Add milk one tablespoon at a time, beating in between additions until at desired consistency. Turn mixer up to medium-high and beat for 1–2 minutes. Fold in quick oats, M&Ms, and mini chocolate chips.

5. Once cupcakes have completely cooled, frost cupcakes with cookie dough frosting using a small ice cream or cookie dough scoop.

Strawberry Princess

STRAWBERRY CUPCAKES

1 box strawberry cake mix

4 Tbsp. instant strawberries & cream pudding

4 large eggs

½ cup sour cream

1 cup milk

¼ cup melted butter (slightly cooled)

STRAWBERRIES & CREAM FILLING

12 Tbsp. instant strawberries & cream pudding

2 cups milk

STRAWBERRY BUTTERCREAM

1 cup unsalted butter

1 cup shortening

3 Tbsp. strawberry extract

8 cups powdered sugar

4–6 Tbsp. milk

pink gel coloring

PARTY-PERFECT

These would also be great served at a baby girl shower or a berry-themed party. Switch out the topper for little baby booties or fondant strawberry tops!

1. Preheat oven to 350 degrees. Line two 12-cup cupcake pans with cupcake liners and set aside.

2. In a medium mixing bowl, sift together cake mix and pudding and set aside. Beat together eggs, sour cream, and milk at low speed. Add dry ingredients and beat until just combined. Beat in melted butter until just combined. Once all ingredients are incorporated, scrape the sides and bottom of the bowl and turn mixer up to medium and beat once more for 15–20 seconds. Do not overbeat.

3. Spoon three tablespoons of batter into each cupcake liner and bake on middle oven rack for 16–18 minutes, baking up to 24 cupcakes side by side at a time. (For best results, bake cupcakes one pan at a time.) Once a toothpick comes out clean, remove from oven and allow cupcakes to rest in pan for 2–4 minutes before removing and transferring to a cooling rack. Prepare pan and repeat this step with any remaining batter.

4. While cupcakes are cooling, prepare filling and buttercream. For strawberry pudding filling, whisk together instant pudding and milk in a small mixing bowl and place in fridge to chill. For strawberry buttercream, in the bowl of a stand mixer (or large mixing bowl) using the paddle attachment, cream butter at medium speed until soft and smooth. Add shortening and strawberry extract and beat until combined. Slowly add in powdered sugar, beating slightly between each addition. Add two tablespoons of milk and small amounts of pink gel coloring until desired color is achieved. Add remaining milk one tablespoon at a time, beating in between additions until at desired consistency. Turn mixer up to medium-high and beat for 1–2 minutes.

5. Once cupcakes have completely cooled, pour and fill cupcakes with strawberry pudding. Frost cupcakes with strawberry buttercream using the traditional swirl technique (page 24) and a large circle tip. Store in an airtight container in the fridge until ready to be served.

PB & J

Cupcakes and kiddos go together like, well, peanut butter and jelly! We love to make these cupcakes for a special after-school treat. Try letting them join in with this recipe; kids make great jelly fillers and peanut sprinklers.

MAKES 24–30 CUPCAKES

WHITE CUPCAKES

1 box white cake mix

4 Tbsp. instant vanilla pudding

4 large egg whites

½ cup sour cream

1¼ cup milk

¼ cup melted butter (slightly cooled)

FILLING

1 cup grape jelly

PEANUT BUTTER FROSTING

1 cup unsalted butter

2 cups smooth peanut butter

1 tsp. vanilla extract

5 cups powdered sugar

5–7 Tbsp. milk

TOPPING

¼ cup chopped peanuts

PARTY-PERFECT

These cupcakes would make a perfect treat for a child's play date. Serve with fresh grapes and milk for the perfect easy setup!

1. Preheat oven to 350 degrees. Line two 12-cup cupcake pans with cupcake liners and set aside.

2. In a medium mixing bowl, sift together cake mix and pudding and set aside. In the bowl of a stand mixer (or large mixing bowl) using the paddle attachment, beat together egg whites, sour cream, and milk at low speed. Add dry ingredients and beat until just combined. Beat in melted butter until just combined. Once all ingredients are incorporated, scrape the sides and bottom of the bowl and turn mixer up to medium and beat once more for 15–20 seconds. Do not overbeat.

3. Spoon three tablespoons of batter into each cupcake liner and bake on middle oven rack for 16–18 minutes, baking up to 24 cupcakes side by side at a time. (For best results, bake cupcakes one pan at a time.) Once a toothpick comes out clean, remove from oven and allow cupcakes to rest in pan for 2–4 minutes before removing and transferring to a cooling rack. Prepare pan and repeat this step with any remaining batter.

4. While cupcakes are cooling, prepare frosting. In the bowl of a stand mixer (or large mixing bowl) using the paddle attachment, cream butter at medium speed until soft and smooth. Add peanut butter and vanilla extract and beat until combined. Slowly add in powdered sugar, beating slightly between each addition. Add milk one tablespoon at a time, beating in between additions until at desired consistency. Turn mixer up to medium-high and beat for 1–2 minutes.

5. Once cupcakes have completed cooled, core and fill cupcakes with grape jelly. Frost cupcakes with peanut butter frosting using the traditional swirl technique (page 24) and a large circle tip. Allow cupcakes to chill for 5 minutes before dipping the top in chopped peanuts.

Bubble Gum

Childhood and bubble gum, there's just no keeping the two separate. Despite how many haircuts it takes, the kiddos love it. They will certainly enjoy devouring these pink bubbly treats with a little gum for after!

MAKES 24–30 CUPCAKES

WHITE CUPCAKES

1 box white cake mix

4 Tbsp. instant vanilla pudding

4 large egg whites

½ cup sour cream

1¼ cup milk

¼ cup melted butter (slightly cooled)

BUBBLE GUM BUTTERCREAM

1 cup unsalted butter

1 cup shortening

1 tsp. vanilla extract

1 dram bubble gum flavoring

8 cups powdered sugar

6–8 Tbsp. milk

pink gel coloring

24–30 gumballs to top

sprinkles to top

MIX IT UP

Rather not give the kids gumballs? No problem! Instead, add some traditional colored nonpareils to the top.

1. Preheat oven to 350 degrees. Line two 12-cup cupcake pans with cupcake liners and set aside.

2. In a medium mixing bowl, sift together cake mix and pudding and set aside. In the bowl of a stand mixer (or large mixing bowl) using the paddle attachment, beat together egg whites, sour cream, and milk at low speed. Add dry ingredients and beat until just combined. Beat in melted butter until just combined. Once all ingredients are incorporated, scrape the sides and bottom of the bowl and turn mixer up to medium and beat once more for 15–20 seconds. Do not overbeat.

3. Spoon three tablespoons of batter into each cupcake liner and bake on middle oven rack for 16–18 minutes, baking up to 24 cupcakes side by side at a time. (For best results, bake cupcakes one pan at a time.) Once a toothpick comes out clean, remove from oven and allow cupcakes to rest in pan for 2–4 minutes before removing and transferring to a cooling rack. Prepare pan and repeat this step with any remaining batter.

4. While cupcakes are cooling, prepare frosting. In the bowl of a stand mixer (or large mixing bowl) using the paddle attachment, cream butter at medium speed until soft and smooth. Add shortening, vanilla extract, and candy flavoring and beat until combined. Slowly add in powdered sugar, beating slightly between each addition. Add two tablespoons of milk and small amounts of pink gel coloring until desired color is achieved. Add remaining milk one tablespoon at a time, beating in between additions until at desired consistency. Turn mixer up to medium-high and beat for 1–2 minutes.

5. Once cupcakes have completely cooled, frost cupcakes with bubble gum buttercream using the traditional swirl technique (page 24) and large circle tip, then top with gumballs and sprinkles if desired.

Dirt Pudding

MAKES 24–30 CUPCAKES

CHOCOLATE CUPCAKES

1 box chocolate cake mix

4 Tbsp. instant chocolate pudding

4 large eggs

½ cup sour cream

1 cup milk

¼ cup melted butter (slightly cooled)

CHOCOLATE PUDDING FILLING

12 Tbsp. instant chocolate pudding

2 cups milk

CHOCOLATE BUTTERCREAM

1 cup unsalted butter

1 cup shortening

1 Tbsp. vanilla extract

8 cups powdered sugar

7 Tbsp. cocoa

6–8 Tbsp. milk

TOPPINGS

½ cup chocolate cookie crumbs

½ cup chocolate rocks

BAKER'S TIP

Find chocolate rocks easily at most local self-serve frozen yogurt bars. They are cheaper and more easily accessible there!

1. Preheat oven to 350 degrees. Line two 12-cup cupcake pans with cupcake liners and set aside.

2. In a medium mixing bowl, sift together cake mix and pudding and set aside. In the bowl of a stand mixer (or large mixing bowl) using the paddle attachment, beat together eggs, sour cream, and milk at low speed. Add dry ingredients and beat until just combined. Beat in melted butter until just combined. Once all ingredients are incorporated, scrape the sides and bottom of the bowl and turn mixer up to medium and beat once more for 15–20 seconds. Do not overbeat.

3. Spoon three tablespoons of batter into each cupcake liner and bake on middle oven rack for 16–18 minutes, baking up to 24 cupcakes side by side at a time. (For best results, bake cupcakes one pan at a time.) Once a toothpick comes out clean, remove from oven and allow cupcakes to rest in pan for 2–4 minutes before removing and transferring to a cooling rack. Prepare pan and repeat this step with any remaining batter.

4. While cupcakes are cooling, prepare chocolate pudding filling and chocolate buttercream. To prepare filling, whisk together instant pudding and milk in a small mixing bowl. Place in fridge to chill. To prepare buttercream, cream butter at medium speed until soft and smooth. Add shortening and vanilla extract and beat until combined. Slowly add in powdered sugar and cocoa, beating slightly between each addition. Add milk one tablespoon at a time, beating in between additions until at desired consistency. Turn mixer up to medium-high and beat for 1–2 minutes.

5. Once cupcakes have completely cooled, core and fill cupcakes with chocolate pudding filling. Frost cupcakes with chocolate buttercream using the traditional swirl technique (page 24) and large round tip. Chill cupcakes for 5 minutes before dipping tops in chocolate cookie crumbs. Place chocolate rocks on top. Store in an airtight container in the fridge until ready to be served.

Cotton Candy

Did you know dreams are made of cupcakes and clouds of cotton candy? It's true! With these fluffy treats, you don't have to be at the fair to enjoy cotton candy anymore. Go ahead and makes those dreams come true!

MAKES 24–30 CUPCAKES

COTTON CANDY CONFFETTI CUPCAKES

1 box white cake mix

4 Tbsp. instant vanilla pudding

4 large egg whites

½ cup sour cream

1¼ cup milk

¼ cup melted butter (slightly cooled)

2 cups cotton candy (compressed and broken into bits)

COTTON CANDY BUTTERCREAM

1 cup unsalted butter

1 cup shortening

1 tsp. vanilla extract

2 packets Duncan Hines Cotton Candy Frosting Creations

8 cups powdered sugar

6–8 Tbsp. milk

MIX IT UP

Cotton Candy Frosting Creation packets can be substituted with 1½ drams of cotton candy candy flavoring and blue gel coloring.

1. Preheat oven to 350 degrees. Line two 12-cup cupcake pans with cupcake liners and set aside.

2. In a medium mixing bowl, sift together cake mix and pudding and set aside. In the bowl of a stand mixer (or large mixing bowl) using the paddle attachment, beat together egg whites, sour cream, and milk at low speed. Add dry ingredients and beat until just combined. Beat in melted butter until just combined. Once all ingredients are incorporated, scrape the sides and bottom of the bowl and turn mixer up to medium and beat once more for 15–20 seconds. Do not overbeat. Fold in cotton candy bits.

3. Spoon three tablespoons of batter into each cupcake liner and bake on middle oven rack for 16–18 minutes, baking up to 24 cupcakes side by side at a time. (For best results, bake cupcakes one pan at a time.) Once a toothpick comes out clean, remove from oven and allow cupcakes to rest in pan for 2–4 minutes before removing and transferring to a cooling rack. Prepare pan and repeat this step with any remaining batter.

4. While cupcakes are cooling, prepare frosting. In the bowl of a stand mixer (or large mixing bowl) using the paddle attachment, cream butter at medium speed until soft and smooth. Add shortening, vanilla extract, and Frosting Creation packets and beat until combined. Slowly add in powdered sugar beating slightly between each addition. Add milk one tablespoon at a time beating in between additions until at desired consistency. Turn mixer up to medium-high and beat for 1–2 minutes.

5. Once cupcakes have completely cooled, frost cupcakes with cotton candy buttercream using the ruffle technique (page 26) and an open star tip. Top with blue candies or pieces of cotton candy just before serving.

Caramel Popcorn

Popcorn! Popcorn! Get your popcorn! Hurry on down and grab one (or two) of these caramel-topped sweets. They'll certainly be the star of the show.

MAKES 24–30 CUPCAKES

YELLOW BUTTERED CUPCAKES

1 box golden butter cake mix

4 Tbsp. instant French vanilla pudding

4 large eggs

½ cup sour cream

1 cup milk

¼ cup melted butter (slightly cooled)

CARAMEL BUTTERCREAM

1 cup unsalted butter

1 cup shortening

2 tsp. caramel extract

1 Tbsp. butter extract

8 cups powdered sugar

pinch of salt

6–8 Tbsp. milk

yellow gel coloring

caramel popcorn to top

TOPPER TIPS

To create these show-worthy toppers, simply hot glue two single tickets to a lollipop stick in a V shape. Tickets can be found at dollar or party stores.

1. Preheat oven to 350 degrees. Line two 12-cup cupcake pans with cupcake liners and set aside.

2. In a medium mixing bowl, sift together cake mix and pudding and set aside. In the bowl of a stand mixer (or large mixing bowl) using the paddle attachment, beat together eggs, sour cream, and milk at low speed. Add dry ingredients and beat until just combined. Beat in melted butter until just combined. Once all ingredients are incorporated, scrape the sides and bottom of the bowl and turn mixer up to medium and beat once more for 15–20 seconds. Do not overbeat.

3. Spoon three tablespoons of batter into each cupcake liner and bake on middle oven rack for 16–18 minutes, baking up to 24 cupcakes side by side at a time. (For best results, bake cupcakes one pan at a time.) Once a toothpick comes out clean, remove from oven and allow cupcakes to rest in pan for 2–4 minutes before removing and transferring to a cooling rack. Prepare pan and repeat this step with any remaining batter.

4. While cupcakes are cooling, prepare frosting. In the bowl of a stand mixer (or large mixing bowl) using the paddle attachment, cream butter at medium speed until soft and smooth. Add shortening and extracts and beat until combined. Slowly add in powdered sugar and salt, beating slightly between each addition. Add two tablespoons of milk and small amounts of yellow gel coloring until desired color is achieved. Add remaining milk one tablespoon at a time, beating in between additions until at desired consistency. Turn mixer up to medium-high and beat for 1–2 minutes.

5. Once cupcakes have cooled, frost cupcakes with caramel buttercream using the traditional swirl technique (page 24) and a large circle tip. Top with caramel popcorn just before serving.

Blue Raspberry

Move over, acrobats. These cupcakes have some real tricks to show off! Your partygoers won't believe just how much these cupcakes look and taste like the real deal. Skip the brain freeze; keep the blue tongue!

MAKES 24–30 CUPCAKES

WHITE CUPCAKES

1 box white cake mix

4 Tbsp. instant vanilla pudding

4 large egg whites

½ cup sour cream

1¼ cup milk

¼ cup melted butter (slightly cooled)

BLUE RASPBERRY BUTTERCREAM

1 cup unsalted butter

1 cup shortening

1 packet blue raspberry Kool-Aid

8 cups powdered sugar

6–8 Tbsp. milk

TOPPING

blue sanding sugar

PARTY-PERFECT

Serve in small snow cone papers, foam cups, or white baking cups, and add a little spoon for the perfect touch!

1. Preheat oven to 350 degrees. Line two 12-cup cupcake pans with cupcake liners and set aside.

2. In a medium mixing bowl, sift together cake mix and pudding and set aside. In the bowl of a stand mixer (or large mixing bowl) using the paddle attachment, beat together eggs, sour cream, and milk at low speed. Add dry ingredients and beat until just combined. Beat in melted butter until just combined. Once all ingredients are incorporated, scrape the sides and bottom of the bowl and turn mixer up to medium and beat once more for 15–20 seconds. Do not overbeat.

3. Spoon three tablespoons of batter into each cupcake liner and bake on middle oven rack for 16–18 minutes, baking up to 24 cupcakes side by side at a time. (For best results, bake cupcakes one pan at a time.) Once a toothpick comes out clean, remove from oven and allow cupcakes to rest in pan for 2–4 minutes before removing and transferring to a cooling rack. Prepare pan and repeat this step with any remaining batter.

4. While cupcakes are cooling, prepare frosting. In the bowl of a stand mixer (or large mixing bowl) using the paddle attachment, cream butter at medium speed until soft and smooth. Add shortening and Kool-Aid packet and beat until combined. Slowly add in powdered sugar, beating slightly between each addition. Add milk one tablespoon at a time, beating in between additions until at desired consistency. Turn mixer up to medium-high and beat for 1–2 minutes.

5. Once cupcakes have completely cooled, scoop frosting onto cupcakes using a small ice cream or cookie dough scoop and smooth with a spatula. Roll in blue sanding sugar and shape with a clean paper towel. For even better results, place in fridge to chill a few minutes before smoothing.

Banana Taffy

If you go bananas over taffy, you will want to give these cupcakes a try
for sure. Despite their soft and fluffy frosting, these taste just like
my favorite banana taffy, and I'm not monkeying around!

MAKES 24–30 CUPCAKES

BANANA CANDY CUPCAKES

1 box yellow cake mix

4 Tbsp. instant banana pudding

4 large eggs

½ cup sour cream

1 cup milk

1 Tbsp. banana extract

¼ cup melted butter (slightly cooled)

BANANA TAFFY BUTTERCREAM

1 cup unsalted butter

1 cup shortening

2 Tbsp. banana extract

8 cups powdered sugar

6–8 Tbsp. milk

yellow gel coloring

TOPPING

banana candies

TOPPER TIPS

Top these cupcakes
with a banana candy, a
twisted banana taffy, or
a banana marshmallow.

1. Preheat oven to 350 degrees. Line two 12-cup cupcake pans with cupcake liners and set aside.

2. In a medium mixing bowl, sift together cake mix and pudding and set aside. In the bowl of a stand mixer (or large mixing bowl) using the paddle attachment, beat together eggs, sour cream, milk, and banana extract at low speed. Add dry ingredients and beat until just combined. Beat in melted butter until just combined. Once all ingredients are incorporated, scrape the sides and bottom of the bowl and turn mixer up to medium and beat once more for 15–20 seconds. Do not overbeat.

3. Spoon three tablespoons of batter into each cupcake liner and bake on middle oven rack for 16–18 minutes, baking up to 24 cupcakes side by side at a time. (For best results, bake cupcakes one pan at a time.) Once a toothpick comes out clean, remove from oven and allow cupcakes to rest in pan for 2–4 minutes before removing and transferring to a cooling rack. Prepare pan and repeat this step with any remaining batter.

4. While cupcakes are cooling, prepare buttercream. In the bowl of a stand mixer (or large mixing bowl) using the paddle attachment, cream butter at medium speed until soft and smooth. Add shortening and banana extract and beat until combined. Slowly add in powdered sugar, beating slightly between each addition. Add two tablespoons of milk and small amounts of yellow gel coloring until desired color is achieved. Add remaining milk one tablespoon at a time, beating in between additions until at desired consistency. Turn mixer up to medium-high and beat for 1–2 minutes.

5. Once cupcakes have completely cooled, frost cupcakes with banana buttercream using the traditional swirl technique (page 24) and a large circle tip. Top with banana candies.

Cake Batter

Sometimes I wonder, why bake a cake when the batter is just as good? With these cupcakes, you can have your cake and batter too. Soft yellow cake with a cake batter–inspired frosting and lots of sprinkles—now that's my kind of cupcake!

MAKES 24–30 CUPCAKES

YELLOW CUPCAKES

1 box yellow cake mix

4 Tbsp. instant vanilla pudding

4 large eggs

½ cup sour cream

1 cup milk

¼ cup melted butter (slightly cooled)

CAKE BATTER FROSTING

1 cup unsalted butter

1 cup shortening

1 tsp. vanilla extract

2 Tbsp. butter extract

6 cups powdered sugar

2 cups sifted yellow cake mix

8–10 Tbsp. milk

SWEET SWIRLS

To add sprinkles as shown, chill cupcakes for a few minutes after the first layer of buttercream and then dip in sprinkles and finish frosting.

1. Preheat oven to 350 degrees. Line two 12-cup cupcake pans with cupcake liners and set aside.

2. In a medium mixing bowl, sift together cake mix and pudding and set aside. In the bowl of a stand mixer (or large mixing bowl) using the paddle attachment, beat together eggs, sour cream, and milk at low speed. Add dry ingredients and beat until just combined. Beat in melted butter until just combined. Once all ingredients are incorporated, scrape the sides and bottom of the bowl and turn mixer up to medium and beat once more for 15–20 seconds. Do not overbeat.

3. Spoon three tablespoons of batter into each cupcake liner and bake on middle oven rack for 16–18 minutes, baking up to 24 cupcakes side by side at a time. (For best results, bake cupcakes one pan at a time.) Once a toothpick comes out clean, remove from oven and allow cupcakes to rest in pan for 2–4 minutes before removing and transferring to a cooling rack. Prepare pan and repeat this step with any remaining batter.

4. While cupcakes are cooling, prepare frosting. In a small mixing bowl sift cake mix and set aside. In the bowl of a stand mixer (or large mixing bowl) using the paddle attachment, cream butter at medium speed until soft and smooth. Add shortening and extracts and beat until combined. Slowly add in powdered sugar and cake mix, beating slightly between each addition. Add milk one tablespoon at a time, beating in between additions until at desired consistency. Turn mixer up to medium-high and beat for 1–2 minutes.

5. Once cupcakes have completely cooled, frost cupcakes with cake batter buttercream using the two-layer effect (page 26) with a large round and open star tip.

Almond Wedding Cake

Move over, cake. Wedding cupcakes are taking center stage at today's trendy weddings. With these little pretties, you can have your cake and your budget too. More for the diamond, of course!

MAKES 24–30 CUPCAKES

WHITE WEDDING CUPCAKES

1 box white cake mix

4 Tbsp. instant vanilla pudding

4 large egg whites

½ cup sour cream

1¼ cup milk

1 Tbsp. almond extract

¼ cup melted butter

ALMOND BUTTERCREAM

1 cup unsalted butter

1 cup shortening

1 Tbsp. almond extract

1 tsp. clear vanilla extract

8 cups powdered sugar

6–8 Tbsp. milk

BAKER'S TIP

Beat frosting really well between each step for a whiter buttercream. To achieve an even whiter look, add a small amount of white gel coloring.

1. Preheat oven to 350 degrees. Line two 12-cup cupcake pans with cupcake liners and set aside.

2. In a medium mixing bowl, sift together cake mix and pudding and set aside. In the bowl of a stand mixer (or large mixing bowl) using the paddle attachment, beat together egg whites, sour cream, and milk at low speed. Add dry ingredients and beat until just combined. Beat in melted butter until just combined. Once all ingredients are incorporated, scrape the sides and bottom of the bowl and turn mixer up to medium and beat once more for 15–20 seconds. Do not overbeat.

3. Spoon three tablespoons of batter into each cupcake liner and bake on middle oven rack for 16–18 minutes, baking up to 24 cupcakes side by side at a time. (For best results, bake cupcakes one pan at a time.) Once a toothpick comes out clean, remove from oven and allow cupcakes to rest in pan for 2–4 minutes before removing and transferring to a cooling rack. Prepare pan and repeat this step with any remaining batter.

4. While cupcakes are cooling, prepare buttercream. In the bowl of a stand mixer (or large mixing bowl) using the paddle attachment, cream butter at medium speed until soft and smooth. Add shortening and extracts and beat until combined. Slowly add in powdered sugar, beating slightly between each addition. Add milk one tablespoon at a time, beating in between additions until at desired consistency. Turn mixer up to medium-high and beat for 1–2 minutes.

5. Once cupcakes completely cooled, frost cupcakes with almond buttercream using the traditional swirl technique (page 24) and a large French star tip.

Pineapple Cream

These cupcakes really are as cute as a button, an edible one even! Soothe those pineapple cravings and welcome the new baby all at once with these fruity treats.

MAKES 24–30 CUPCAKES

PINEAPPLE CUPCAKES

1 box pineapple cake mix

4 Tbsp. instant vanilla pudding

3 large eggs

½ cup sour cream

1 cup pineapple juice

¼ melted butter (slightly cooled)

PINEAPPLE CREAM FROSTING

1 cup unsalted butter

1 cup shortening

1 tsp. vanilla extract

8 cups powdered sugar

2 Tbsp. milk

5–7 Tbsp. pineapple juice

FILLING

1½ cup crushed pineapple

TOPPER TIPS

You can easily recreate these button toppers by cutting out circles using different size frosting tips. Use smaller tips and openings to create the lines inside.

1. Preheat oven to 350 degrees. Line two 12-cup cupcake pans with cupcake liners and set aside.

2. In a medium mixing bowl, sift together cake mix and pudding and set aside. In the bowl of a stand mixer (or large mixing bowl) using the paddle attachment, beat together eggs, sour cream, and pineapple juice at low speed. Add dry ingredients and beat until just combined. Beat in melted butter until just combined. Once all ingredients are incorporated, scrape the sides and bottom of the bowl and turn mixer up to medium and beat once more for 15–20 seconds. Do not overbeat.

3. Spoon three tablespoons of batter into each cupcake liner and bake on middle oven rack for 16–18 minutes, baking up to 24 cupcakes side by side at a time. (For best results, bake cupcakes one pan at a time.) Once a toothpick comes out clean, remove from oven and allow cupcakes to rest in pan for 2–4 minutes before removing and transferring to a cooling rack. Prepare pan and repeat this step with any remaining batter.

4. While cupcakes are cooling, prepare frosting. In the bowl of a stand mixer (or large mixing bowl) using the paddle attachment, cream butter at medium speed until soft and smooth. Add shortening and vanilla extract and beat until combined. Slowly add in powdered sugar, beating slightly between each addition. Add milk and pineapple juice one tablespoon at a time, beating in between additions until at desired consistency. Turn mixer up to medium-high and beat for 2–3 minutes.

5. Once cupcakes have completely cooled, frost cupcakes with pineapple frosting using the ruffle tehnique (page 26) and a large open star tip.

Chocolate Confetti

Why is confetti cake always made with vanilla? Chocolate loves sprinkles too!
Besides, other than sprinkles, how else could you really improve chocolate?
(Besides adding more chocolate, of course.)

MAKES 24–30 CUPCAKES

CHOCOLATE CONFETTI CUPCAKES

1 box milk chocolate cake mix

4 Tbsp. instant chocolate pudding

4 large eggs

½ cup sour cream

1 cup milk

¼ melted butter (slightly cooled)

½ cup rainbow sprinkles

CHOCOLATE BUTTERCREAM

1 cup unsalted butter

1 cup shortening

1 Tbsp. vanilla extract

8 cups powdered sugar

7 Tbsp. cocoa

6–8 Tbsp. milk

TOPPING

¼ cup rainbow sprinkles

MIX IT UP

Turn these into a triple chocolate rainbow treat by drizzling a little chocolate ganache (page 122) on top.

1. In a medium mixing bowl, sift together cake mix and pudding and set aside. In the bowl of a stand mixer (or large mixing bowl) using the paddle attachment, beat together eggs, sour cream, and milk at low speed. Add dry ingredients and beat until just combined. Beat in melted butter until just combined. Once all ingredients are incorporated, scrape the sides and bottom of the bowl and turn mixer up to medium and beat once more for 15–20 seconds. Do not overbeat. Fold in sprinkles.

2. Spoon three tablespoons of batter into each cupcake liner and bake on middle oven rack for 16–18 minutes, baking up to 24 cupcakes side by side at a time. (For best results, bake cupcakes one pan at a time.) Once a toothpick comes out clean, remove from oven and allow cupcakes to rest in pan for 2–4 minutes before removing and transferring to a cooling rack. Prepare pan and repeat this step with any remaining batter.

3. While cupcakes are cooling, prepare chocolate buttercream. In the bowl of a stand mixer (or large mixing bowl) using the paddle attachment, cream butter at medium speed until soft and smooth. Add shortening and vanilla extract and beat until combined. Slowly add in powdered sugar and cocoa, beating slightly between each addition. Add milk one tablespoon at a time, beating in between additions until at desired consistency. Turn mixer up to medium-high and beat for 1–2 minutes.

4. Once cupcakes have completely cooled, frost cupcakes with chocolate buttercream using traditional swirl techniques (page 24) and an open star tip. Top with sprinkles.

Very Vanilla

Sometimes sweet and simple is the way to go, and you definitely can't go wrong with these swirls of vanilla. Cover them in sprinkles or top them with candles; they're the perfect blank canvas to any occasion!

MAKES 24–30 CUPCAKES

FRENCH VANILLA CUPCAKES

1 box French vanilla cake mix

4 Tbsp. instant French vanilla pudding

4 large egg whites

½ cup sour cream

1¼ cup milk

¼ cup melted butter (slightly cooled)

VANILLA BUTTERCREAM

1 cup unsalted butter

1 cup shortening

1 Tbsp. clear vanilla extract

8 cups powdered sugar

6–8 Tbsp. milk

TOPPING

sprinkles

MIX IT UP

Turn these into confetti cupcakes by folding in ¼–½ cup of sprinkles just after mixing the batter.

1. Preheat oven to 350 degrees. Line two 12-cup cupcake pans with cupcake liners and set aside.

2. In a medium mixing bowl, sift together cake mix and pudding and set aside. In the bowl of a stand mixer (or large mixing bowl) using the paddle attachment, beat together egg whites, sour cream, and milk at low speed. Add dry ingredients and beat until just combined. Beat in melted butter until just combined. Once all ingredients are incorporated, scrape the sides and bottom of the bowl and turn mixer up to medium and beat once more for 15–20 seconds. Do not overbeat.

3. Spoon three tablespoons of batter into each cupcake liner and bake on middle oven rack for 16–18 minutes, baking up to 24 cupcakes side by side at a time. (For best results, bake cupcakes one pan at a time.) Once a toothpick comes out clean, remove from oven and allow cupcakes to rest in pan for 2–4 minutes before removing and transferring to a cooling rack. Prepare pan and repeat this step with any remaining batter.

4. While cupcakes are cooling, prepare vanilla buttercream. In the bowl of a stand mixer (or large mixing bowl) using the paddle attachment, cream butter at medium speed until soft and smooth. Add shortening and vanilla extract and beat until combined. Slowly add in powdered sugar, beating slightly between each addition. Add milk one tablespoon at a time, beating in between additions until at desired consistency. Turn mixer up to medium-high and beat for 1–2 minutes.

5. Once cupcakes have completely cooled, frost cupcakes with vanilla buttercream using the traditional swirl technique (page 24) and a large circle tip. Top with sprinkles if desired.

Seasonal Celebrations

White Chocolate Raspberry

Is there really a better way to start off the year than by having a little white chocolate? Nope, not that I can think of! But don't worry, you'll soon be finding excuses to make these all year round.

MAKES 24–30 CUPCAKES

WHITE CHOCOLATE CUPCAKES

1 box white cake mix

4 Tbsp. instant white chocolate pudding

4 large egg whites

½ cup sour cream

1¼ cup milk

¼ cup melted butter (slightly cooled)

FILLING

1 (21-oz.) jar raspberry jam

WHITE CHOCOLATE FROSTING

8 oz. white melting chocolate

1 cup unsalted butter

1 tsp. vanilla extract

4 cups powdered sugar

2–3 Tbsp. heavy cream (or milk)

MIX IT UP

Raspberry pie filling can be used in place of raspberry jam to fill cupcakes; however, cupcakes will needed to be stored in fridge and then frosted just before serving.

1. Preheat oven to 350 degrees. Line two 12-cup cupcake pans with cupcake liners and set aside.

2. In a medium mixing bowl, sift together cake mix and pudding and set aside. In the bowl of a stand mixer (or large mixing bowl) using the paddle attachment, beat together egg whites, sour cream, and milk at low speed. Add dry ingredients and beat until just combined. Beat in melted butter until just combined. Once all ingredients are incorporated, scrape the sides and bottom of the bowl and turn mixer up to medium and beat once more for 15–20 seconds. Do not overbeat.

3. Spoon three tablespoons of batter into each cupcake liner and bake on middle oven rack for 16–18 minutes, baking up to 24 cupcakes side by side at a time. Once toothpick comes out clean, remove from oven and allow cupcakes to rest for 2 minutes before removing and transferring them to a cooling rack. Prepare and bake additional cupcakes with any remaining batter.

4. While cupcakes are cooling, prepare frosting. In a small glass bowl, melt white chocolate in the microwave 30 seconds at a time, stirring in between until smooth. Once white chocolate has slightly cooled, in the bowl of a stand mixer (or large mixing bowl) using the paddle attachment, cream butter at medium speed until soft and smooth. Add melted chocolate and vanilla extract and beat until combined. Slowly add in powdered sugar, beating slightly between each addition. Add cream one tablespoon at a time, beating in between additions until at desired consistency. Turn mixer up to medium-high and beat for 1–2 minutes.

5. Once cupcakes have completely cooled, core and fill with raspberry filling. Frost cupcakes with white chocolate frosting using the traditional swirl technique (page 24) and a large circle tip. Store airtight container on counter. Do not refrigerate. (White chocolate frosting will harden in fridge.)

Strawberry Chocolate

Show them just how much you love them with this perfect Valentine's Day combo: chocolate and strawberry! Before you know it, you'll have more valentines than you have cupcakes.

MAKES 24–30 CUPCAKES

CHOCOLATE CUPCAKES

1 box chocolate cake mix

4 Tbsp. instant chocolate pudding

4 large eggs

½ cup sour cream

1 cup milk

¼ cup melted butter (slightly cooled)

FILLING

12 Tbsp. instant chocolate pudding

2 cups milk

½ cup diced strawberries

STRAWBERRY BUTTERCREAM

1 cup unsalted butter

1 cup shortening

2 Tbsp. strawberry extract

8 cups powdered sugar

6–8 Tbsp. milk

pink gel coloring

heart sprinkles to top

SWEET SWIRLS

For this two-layer frosting, use a large circle tip (Wilton 2A) on bottom and a open star tip (Wilton 1M) on top.

1. Preheat oven to 350 degrees. Line two 12-cup cupcake pans with cupcake liners and set aside.

2. In a medium mixing bowl, sift together cake mix and pudding and set aside. In the bowl of a stand mixer (or large mixing bowl) using the paddle attachment, beat together eggs, sour cream, and milk at low speed. Add dry ingredients and beat until just combined. Beat in melted butter until just combined. Once all ingredients are incorporated, scrape the sides and bottom of the bowl and turn mixer up to medium and beat once more for 15–20 seconds. Do not overbeat.

3. Spoon three tablespoons of batter into each cupcake liner and bake on middle oven rack for 16–18 minutes, baking up to 24 cupcakes side by side at a time. (For best results, bake cupcakes one pan at a time.) Once a toothpick comes out clean, remove from oven and allow cupcakes to rest in pan for 2–4 minutes before removing and transferring to a cooling rack. Prepare pan and repeat this step with any remaining batter.

4. While cupcakes are cooling, prepare filling and buttercream. To prepare filling whisk together pudding, milk, and strawberries in a small mixing bowl. Place in fridge to chill. To prepare buttercream, in the bowl of a stand mixer (or large mixing bowl) using the paddle attachment, cream butter at medium speed until soft and smooth. Add shortening and strawberry extract and beat until combined. Slowly add in powdered sugar, beating slightly between each addition. Beat in two tablespoons of milk and small amounts of pink gel coloring until desired color is achieved. Then add remaining milk one tablespoon at a time, beating in between each addition until at desired consistency scraping bowl in between to incorporate color evenly.

5. Once cupcakes have completely cooled, core and fill with chocolate pudding filling. Frost cupcakes with strawberry buttercream using the two-layer effect (page 27) and the large circle and open star tips. Top with a heart sprinkle if desired.

Red Velvet Cheesecake

Flowers—who needs 'em? Celebrate Valentine's Day with a dozen of these oh-so-lovely cupcakes instead. With a soft red velvet cake and a creamy cheesecake frosting, you won't even need the box of chocolates!

MAKES 24–30 CUPCAKES

RED VELVET CUPCAKES

1 box red velvet cake mix

4 Tbsp. instant chocolate pudding

4 large eggs

½ cup sour cream

1 cup buttermilk

¼ cup melted butter (slightly cooled)

CHEESECAKE FROSTING

4 Tbsp. instant cheesecake pudding

1 cup unsalted butter

1 (8-oz.) pkg. cream cheese

1 tsp. vanilla extract

5 cups powdered sugar

3–5 Tbsp. milk

SWEET SWIRLS

Turn the frosting into a rose itself by using the cinnamon roll technique and a Wilton 2A tip.

1. Preheat oven to 350 degrees. Line two 12-cup cupcake pans with cupcake liners and set aside.

2. In a medium mixing bowl, sift together cake mix and pudding and set aside. In the bowl of a stand mixer (or large mixing bowl) using the paddle attachment, beat together eggs, sour cream, and buttermilk at low speed. Add dry ingredients and beat until just combined. Beat in melted butter until just combined. Once all ingredients are incorporated, scrape the sides and bottom of the bowl and turn mixer up to medium and beat once more for 15–20 seconds. Do not overbeat.

3. Spoon three tablespoons of batter into each cupcake liner and bake on middle oven rack for 16–18 minutes, baking up to 24 cupcakes side by side at a time. (For best results, bake cupcakes one pan at a time.) Once a toothpick comes out clean, remove from oven and allow cupcakes to rest in pan for 2–4 minutes before removing and transferring to a cooling rack. Prepare pan and repeat this step with any remaining batter.

4. While cupcakes are cooling, prepare frosting. In a small bowl mix together pudding and four tablespoons of milk and set aside. In the bowl of a stand mixer (or large mixing bowl) using the paddle attachment, cream butter at medium speed until soft and smooth. Add cream cheese and vanilla extract and beat until combined. Slowly add in powdered sugar, beating slightly between each addition. Add pudding and then milk one tablespoon at a time, beating in between additions until at desired consistency. Turn mixer up to medium-high and beat for 1–2 minutes.

5. Once cupcakes have completely cooled, frost cupcakes using traditional swirl technique (page 24) and a closed star tip. Store in an airtight container and refrigerate until served.

Green Velvet Butterscotch

MAKES 24–30 CUPCAKES

GREEN VELVET CUPCAKES

1 box yellow cake mix

4 Tbsp. instant butterscotch pudding

4 large eggs

½ cup sour cream

1 cup buttermilk

¼ cup melted butter (slightly cooled)

green gel coloring

BUTTERSCOTCH FROSTING

12 Tbsp. instant butterscotch pudding

1 cup unsalted butter

1 cup shortening

1 tsp. vanilla extract

8 cups powdered sugar

8–10 Tbsp. milk

BUTTERSCOTCH GANACHE

4 Tbsp. heavy cream

2 cups butterscotch chips

BAKER'S TIP

To make buttermilk at home, add one tablespoon of white vinegar to one cup of milk and let sit for 20 minutes.

1. Preheat oven to 350 degrees. Line two 12-cup cupcake pans with cupcake liners and set aside.

2. In a medium mixing bowl, sift together cake mix and pudding and set aside. In the bowl of a stand mixer (or large mixing bowl) using the paddle attachment, beat together eggs, sour cream, buttermilk, and a small amount of green gel coloring at low speed. Add dry ingredients and beat until just combined. Beat in melted butter until just combined. If green color is not strong enough add additional green gel coloring. Once all ingredients are incorporated, scrape the sides and bottom of the bowl and turn mixer up to medium and beat once more for 15–20 seconds. Do not overbeat.

3. Spoon three tablespoons of batter into each cupcake liner and bake on middle oven rack for 16–18 minutes, baking up to 24 cupcakes side by side at a time. (For best results, bake cupcakes one pan at a time.) Once a toothpick comes out clean, remove from oven and allow cupcakes to rest in pan for 2–4 minutes before removing and transferring to a cooling rack. Prepare pan and repeat this step with any remaining batter.

4. While cupcakes are cooling, prepare ganache and frosting. To prepare ganache, microwave heavy cream in a small glass bowl for 30 seconds. Stir in butterscotch chips until almost smooth and place back in microwave for 30 seconds. Stir until smooth and then set aside to cool. To prepare buttercream, whisk together butterscotch pudding and four tablespoons of milk in a bowl; set aside. In the bowl of a stand mixer (or large mixing bowl) using the paddle attachment, cream butter at medium speed until soft and smooth. Add shortening and extract and beat until combined. Slowly add in powdered sugar, beating slightly between each addition. Add butterscotch pudding and add remaining milk one tablespoon at a time, until at desired consistency. Turn mixer up to medium-high and beat for 1–2 minutes.

5. Once cupcakes have completely cooled, frost cupcakes with butterscotch frosting using the traditional swirl technique (page 24) and a open star tip (Wilton 1M); then pipe or spoon ganache on to tops of cupcakes.

Chocolate Caramel Irish Cream

You won't need a rainbow or a leprechaun to enjoy this pot of gold. The Irish cream, buttercream, and caramel-soaked cake will hit the spot. You might even dance a little jig!

MAKES 24–30 CUPCAKES

CHOCOLATE CUPCAKES

1 box devil's food cake mix

4 Tbsp. instant chocolate pudding mix

4 large eggs

½ cup sour cream

1 cup coffee (slightly cooled)

¼ cup melted butter (slightly cooled)

FILLING

1 cup caramel topping

IRISH CREAM BUTTERCREAM

2 cups unsalted butter

1 tsp. vanilla extract

2 Tbsp. caramel topping

8 cups powdered sugar

6–8 Tbsp. Irish cream coffee creamer

TOPPER TIPS

To make these simple toppers, cut small hearts and stems from green fondant. "Glue" together with a small amount of warm water and let dry for several hours.

1. Preheat oven to 350 degrees. Line two 12-cup cupcake pans with cupcake liners and set aside.

2. In a medium mixing bowl, sift together cake mix and pudding and set aside. In the bowl of a stand mixer (or large mixing bowl) using the paddle attachment, beat together eggs, sour cream, and coffee at low speed. Add dry ingredients and beat until just combined. Beat in melted butter until just combined. Once all ingredients are incorporated, scrape the sides and bottom of the bowl and turn mixer up to medium and beat once more for 15–20 seconds. Do not overbeat.

3. Spoon three tablespoons of batter into each cupcake liner and bake on middle oven rack for 16–18 minutes, baking up to 24 cupcakes side by side at a time. (For best results, bake cupcakes one pan at a time.) Once a toothpick comes out clean, remove from oven and allow cupcakes to rest in pan for 2–4 minutes before removing and transferring to a cooling rack. Prepare pan and repeat this step with any remaining batter.

4. While cupcakes are cooling, prepare buttercream. In the bowl of a stand mixer (or large mixing bowl) using the paddle attachment, cream butter at medium speed until soft and smooth. Add vanilla extract and caramel and beat until combined. Slowly add in powdered sugar, beating slightly between each addition. Add creamer one tablespoon at a time, beating in between additions until at desired consistency. Turn mixer up to medium-high and beat for 1–2 minutes.

5. Once cupcakes have completely cooled, core them, keeping the tops to use. Fill cupcakes with caramel topping and replace tops back on cupcakes. (Some caramel will absorb.) Frost cupcakes with Irish cream buttercream using the traditional swirl technique (page 24) and a jumbo circle tip. Sprinkle with gold sprinkles or coins if desired.

German Chocolate Coconut Almond

Don't you love it when a cupcake is just as cute as it is delicious? With that fuzzy little bunny disguise, you almost won't want to indulge in the coconut almond buttercream inside … almost.

MAKES 24–30 CUPCAKES

GERMAN CHOCOLATE CAKE

1 box German chocolate cake mix

4 Tbsp. instant chocolate pudding

4 large eggs

½ cup sour cream

1 cup milk

¼ cup melted butter (slightly cooled)

COCONUT ALMOND BUTTERCREAM

1 cup unsalted butter

1 cup shortening

1 Tbsp. coconut extract

1 tsp. almond extract

8 cups powdered sugar

6–8 tbsp. milk

TOPPINGS

2 cups coconut flakes

white Jordan almonds

BAKER'S TIP

To create a nice smooth top, chill cupcakes after adding coconut. After a few minutes, you will be able to shape the frosting with a paper towel.

1. Preheat oven to 350 degrees. Line two 12-cup cupcake pans with cupcake liners and set aside.

2. In a medium mixing bowl, sift together cake mix and pudding and set aside. In the bowl of a stand mixer (or large mixing bowl) using the paddle attachment, beat together eggs, sour cream, and milk at low speed. Add dry ingredients and beat until just combined. Beat in melted butter until just combined. Once all ingredients are incorporated, scrape the sides and bottom of the bowl and turn mixer up to medium and beat once more for 15–20 seconds. Do not overbeat.

3. Spoon three tablespoons of batter into each cupcake liner and bake on middle oven rack for 16–18 minutes, baking up to 24 cupcakes side by side at a time. (For best results, bake cupcakes one pan at a time.) Once a toothpick comes out clean, remove from oven and allow cupcakes to rest in pan for 2–4 minutes before removing and transferring to a cooling rack. Prepare pan and repeat this step with any remaining batter.

4. Once cupcakes have been removed from the oven, spread coconut flakes in a thin layer across a cookie sheet. Bake at 350 degrees for 4–5 minutes. Coconut flakes should be crisp but not yet browned. Transfer to a bowl and let cool.

5. While cupcakes and coconut flakes are cooling, prepare buttercream. In the bowl of a stand mixer (or large mixing bowl) using the paddle attachment, cream butter at medium speed until soft and smooth. Add shortening and extracts and beat until combined. Slowly add in powdered sugar, beating slightly between each addition. Add milk one tablespoon at a time, beating in between additions until at desired consistency. Turn mixer up to medium-high and beat for 1–2 minutes.

6. Once cupcakes have completely cooled, frost cupcakes with coconut almond buttercream using the traditional swirl technique (page 24) and a large circle tip. Then cover in crisped coconut flakes. Place white Jordan almonds on top for ears.

Lemon Pudding

I like to say the only green thumb I have comes from food coloring.
So the only flowers I grow are edible ones. What better way to say
"spring is in the air" than by baking a fresh garden of cupcakes?

MAKES 24–30 CUPCAKES

LEMON CUPCAKES

1 box lemon cake mix

4 Tbsp. instant lemon pudding

4 large eggs

½ cup sour cream

1 cup milk

¼ cup melted butter
(slightly cooled)

FILLING

12 Tbsp. instant lemon pudding

2 cups milk

LEMON BUTTERCREAM

1 cup unsalted butter

1 cup shortening

2 Tbsp. lemon extract

1 tsp. vanilla extract

8 cups powdered sugar

6–8 Tbsp. milk

yellow gel coloring

TOPPER TIP

Glue paper flowers
to green paper straw
stems for a tall garden
of cupcakes to serve.

1. Preheat oven to 350 degrees. Line two 12-cup cupcake pans with cupcake liners and set aside.

2. In a medium mixing bowl, sift together cake mix and pudding and set aside. In the bowl of a stand mixer (or large mixing bowl) using the paddle attachment, beat together eggs, sour cream, and milk at low speed. Add dry ingredients and beat until just combined. Beat in melted butter until just combined. Once all ingredients are incorporated, scrape the sides and bottom of the bowl and turn mixer up to medium and beat once more for 15–20 seconds. Do not overbeat.

3. Spoon three tablespoons of batter into each cupcake liner and bake on middle oven rack for 16–18 minutes, baking up to 24 cupcakes side by side at a time. (For best results, bake cupcakes one pan at a time.) Once a toothpick comes out clean, remove from oven and allow cupcakes to rest in pan for 2–4 minutes before removing and transferring to a cooling rack. Prepare pan and repeat this step with any remaining batter.

4. While cupcakes are cooling, prepare filling and buttercream. To prepare filling, whisk together instant pudding and milk in a small mixing bowl. Place in fridge to chill. To prepare buttercream in the bowl of a stand mixer (or large mixing bowl) using the paddle attachment, cream butter at medium speed until soft and smooth. Add shortening and extracts and beat until combined. Slowly add in powdered sugar, beating slightly between each addition. Add two tablespoons of milk and small amounts of yellow gel coloring until desired color is achieved. Add remaining milk one tablespoon at a time, beating in between additions until at desired consistency. Turn mixer up to medium-high and beat for 1–2 minutes.

5. Once cupcakes have completely cooled, core and fill cupcakes with lemon pudding. Frost cupcakes with lemon buttercream using the traditional swirl technique (page 24) and large circle tip. Store in an airtight container and refrigerate until served. Top with premade flowers just before serving.

Cherry Almond Flowers

Everybody knows moms can't resist flowers, especially ones made of buttercream and sprinkles. Let your mom know just how special she is with a batch of these flowers—you'll be the favorite for sure!

MAKES 24–30 CUPCAKES

CHERRY CUPCAKES

1 cherry chip cake mix

4 Tbsp. instant French vanilla pudding

4 large eggs

½ cup sour cream

1 cup milk

¼ cup butter (slightly cooled)

CHERRY ALMOND BUTTERCREAM

1 cup unsalted butter

1 cup shortening

1 Tbsp. cherry extract

1 Tbsp. almond extract

8 cups powdered sugar

6–8 Tbsp. milk

pink gel coloring

TOPPINGS

cherry candy centers or sprinkled candy melt centers

TOPPER TIPS

Create these sprinkle centers by melting circle candy melts in the oven for a few moments on a cookie sheet lined with parchment paper. Remove and cover with sprinkles, then let cool.

1. Preheat oven to 350 degrees. Line two 12-cup cupcake pans with cupcake liners and set aside.

2. In a medium mixing bowl, sift together cake mix and pudding and set aside. In the bowl of a stand mixer (or large mixing bowl) using the paddle attachment, beat together eggs, sour cream, and milk at low speed. Add dry ingredients and beat until just combined. Beat in melted butter until just combined. Once all ingredients are incorporated, scrape the sides and bottom of the bowl and turn mixer up to medium and beat once more for 15–20 seconds. Do not overbeat.

3. Spoon three tablespoons of batter into each cupcake liner and bake on middle oven rack for 16–18 minutes, baking up to 24 cupcakes side by side at a time. (For best results, bake cupcakes one pan at a time.) Once a toothpick comes out clean, remove from oven and allow cupcakes to rest in pan for 2–4 minutes before removing and transferring to a cooling rack. Prepare pan and repeat this step with any remaining batter.

4. While cupcakes are cooling, prepare frosting. In the bowl of a stand mixer (or large mixing bowl) using the paddle attachment, cream butter at medium speed until soft and smooth. Add shortening and extracts and beat until combined. Slowly add in powdered sugar, beating slightly between each addition. Add two tablespoons of milk and small amounts of pink gel coloring until desired color is achieved. Add remaining milk one tablespoon at a time, beating in until at desired consistency. Turn mixer up to medium-high and beat for one minute.

5. Once cupcakes have completely cooled, frost cupcakes with cherry almond buttercream using the flower petal technique (page 24) and a large circle tip. Add candy center to finish flower.

Watermelon

It isn't summer without watermelon and it isn't a party without cake.
Why not combined the two for the coolest of summer treats?

MAKES 24–30 CUPCAKES

VANILLA CUPCAKES

1 box white cake mix
4 Tbsp. instant vanilla pudding
4 large egg whites
½ cup sour cream
1¼ cup milk
red gel coloring
¼ cup black sprinkles

WATERMELON BUTTERCREAM

1 cup unsalted butter
1 cup shortening
1 watermelon Kool-Aid packet
8 cups powdered sugar
6–8 Tbsp. milk
red gel coloring
¼ cup black sprinkles

TOPPER TIPS

Ants really make these cupcakes into a fun treat. You can often find little ant sprinkles with Halloween sprinkles.

1. Preheat oven to 350 degrees. Line two 12-cup cupcake pans with cupcake liners and set aside.

2. In a medium mixing bowl, sift together cake mix and pudding and set aside. In the bowl of a stand mixer (or large mixing bowl) using the paddle attachment, beat together egg whites, sour cream, and milk and a small amount of red gel coloring at low speed. Add dry ingredients and beat until just combined. Beat in melted butter until just combined. If red color is not strong enough, mix in a little more coloring. Once all ingredients are incorporated, scrape the sides and bottom of the bowl and turn mixer up to medium and beat once more for 15–20 seconds. Do not overbeat. Fold in black sprinkles.

3. Spoon three tablespoons of batter into each cupcake liner and bake on middle oven rack for 16–18 minutes, baking up to 24 cupcakes side by side at a time. (For best results, bake cupcakes one pan at a time.) Once a toothpick comes out clean, remove from oven and allow cupcakes to rest in pan for 2–4 minutes before removing and transferring to a cooling rack. Prepare pan and repeat this step with any remaining batter.

4. While cupcakes are cooling, prepare buttercream. In the bowl of a stand mixer (or large mixing bowl) using the paddle attachment, cream butter at medium speed until soft and smooth. Add shortening and Kool-Aid packets and beat until combined. Slowly add in powdered sugar, beating slightly between each addition. Add two tablespoons of milk and small amounts of red gel coloring until desired color is achieved. Turn mixer up to medium-high and beat for 1–2 minutes.

5. Once cupcakes have completely cooled, frost cupcakes with watermelon buttercream using the traditional swirl technique (page 24) and a large circle tip.

Mint Chocolate

Fore! No really, you're going to have to stop yourself at four,
because these cupcakes are such a hole in one!

MAKES 24–30 CUPCAKES

DEVIL'S FOOD CUPCAKES

1 box devil's food cake mix

4 Tbsp. instant chocolate pudding

4 large eggs

½ cup sour cream

1 cup milk

¼ cup melted butter (slightly cooled)

MINT CREAM FROSTING

1 cup unsalted butter

1 (8-oz.) pkg. cream cheese

1 Tbsp. mint extract

1 tsp. vanilla extract

6 cups powdered sugar

4–6 Tbsp. milk

green gel coloring

MIX IT UP

These cupcakes not only make the perfect Father's Day treat, but they would also be cute spruced up for St. Patrick's Day or Christmas!

1. Preheat oven to 350 degrees. Line two 12-cup cupcake pans with cupcake liners and set aside.

2. In a medium mixing bowl, sift together cake mix and pudding and set aside. In the bowl of a stand mixer (or large mixing bowl) using the paddle attachment, beat together eggs, sour cream, and milk at low speed. Add dry ingredients and beat until just combined. Beat in melted butter until just combined. Once all ingredients are incorporated, scrape the sides and bottom of the bowl and turn mixer up to medium and beat once more for 15–20 seconds. Do not overbeat.

3. Spoon three tablespoons of batter into each cupcake liner and bake on middle oven rack for 16–18 minutes, baking up to 24 cupcakes side by side at a time. (For best results, bake cupcakes one pan at a time.) Once a toothpick comes out clean, remove from oven and allow cupcakes to rest in pan for 2–4 minutes before removing and transferring to a cooling rack. Prepare pan and repeat this step with any remaining batter.

4. While cupcakes are cooling, prepare frosting. In the bowl of a stand mixer (or large mixing bowl) using the paddle attachment, cream butter at medium speed until soft and smooth. Add cream cheese and extracts and beat until combined. Slowly add in powdered sugar, beating slightly between each addition. Add two tablespoons of milk and a small amount of green gel coloring until desired color is achieved. Add remaining milk one tablespoon at a time, beating until at desired consistency. Turn mixer up to medium-high and beat for one minute.

5. Once cupcakes have completely cooled, frost cupcakes with mint cream buttercream using a grass tip. Simply cover the cupcake by piping on small "blades of grass." Place piping tip just above cupcake, apply pressure, and then release and pull up. Store in an airtight container and refrigerate until served.

Patriotic Apple Pie

Create a real spark this year with this cupcake version of a patriotic treat—apple pie! Enjoy them at your backyard barbecue or right under the fireworks.

MAKES 24–30 CUPCAKES

VANILLA CUPCAKES

1 box white cake mix

4 Tbsp. instant vanilla pudding

4 large egg whites

½ cup sour cream

1¼ cup milk

¼ cup melted butter (slightly cooled)

FILLING

1 can apple pie filling (cut into small chunks)

CINNAMON VANILLA BUTTERCREAM

1 cup unsalted butter

1 cup shortening

1 Tbsp. vanilla extract

½ tsp. cinnamon

8 cups powdered sugar

6–8 Tbsp. milk

PARTY-PERFECT

Create a sweet Fourth of July spark by adding sparklers to the top of the cupcakes and lighting just before serving.

1. Preheat oven to 350 degrees. Line two 12-cup cupcake pans with cupcake liners and set aside.

2. In a medium mixing bowl, sift together cake mix and pudding and set aside. In the bowl of a stand mixer (or large mixing bowl) using the paddle attachment, beat together egg whites, sour cream, and milk at low speed. Add dry ingredients and beat until just combined. Beat in melted butter until just combined. Once all ingredients are incorporated, scrape the sides and bottom of the bowl and turn mixer up to medium and beat once more for 15–20 seconds. Do not overbeat.

3. Spoon three tablespoons of batter into each cupcake liner and bake on middle oven rack for 16–18 minutes, baking up to 24 cupcakes side by side at a time. (For best results, bake cupcakes one pan at a time.) Once a toothpick comes out clean, remove from oven and allow cupcakes to rest in pan for 2–4 minutes before removing and transferring to a cooling rack. Prepare pan and repeat this step with any remaining batter.

4. While cupcakes are cooling, prepare buttercream. In the bowl of a stand mixer (or large mixing bowl) using the paddle attachment, cream butter at medium speed until soft and smooth. Add shortening, vanilla extract, and cinnamon and beat until combined. Slowly add in powdered sugar, beating slightly between each addition. Add milk one tablespoon at a time, beating in between additions until at desired consistency. Turn mixer up to medium-high and beat for 1–2 minutes.

5. Once cupcakes have completely cooled, core and fill with apple pie filling. Frost cupcakes with cinnamon vanilla buttercream using traditional swirl technique (page 24) and closed star tip. Store in an airtight container and refrigerate until served.

Neapolitan

MILK CHOCOLATE CUPCAKES

1 box milk chocolate cake mix

4 Tbsp. instant milk chocolate pudding

4 large eggs

½ cup sour cream

1 cup milk

¼ cup melted butter (slightly cooled)

NEAPOLITAN BUTTERCREAM

1 cup unsalted butter

1 cup shortening

1 Tbsp. vanilla extract

8 cups powdered sugar

6–7 Tbsp. milk

2½ Tbsp. cocoa powder

2 tsp. strawberry extract

pink gel coloring

chopped peanuts to top

candy cherries to top

MIX IT UP

For a real cone look, line ice cream cones up on a cookie sheet and bake the cake mix right inside the cone.

1. Preheat oven to 350 degrees. Line two 12-cup cupcake pans with cupcake liners and set aside.

2. In a medium mixing bowl, sift together cake mix and pudding and set aside. Beat together eggs, sour cream, and milk at low speed. Add dry ingredients and beat until just combined. Beat in melted butter until just combined. Once all ingredients are incorporated, scrape the sides and bottom of the bowl and turn mixer up to medium and beat once more for 15–20 seconds. Do not overbeat.

3. Spoon three tablespoons of batter into each cupcake liner and bake on middle oven rack for 16–18 minutes, baking up to 24 cupcakes side by side at a time. (For best results, bake cupcakes one pan at a time.) Once a toothpick comes out clean, remove from oven and allow cupcakes to rest in pan for 2–4 minutes before removing and transferring to a cooling rack. Prepare pan and repeat this step with any remaining batter.

4. While cupcakes are cooling, prepare buttercream. Cream butter at medium speed until soft and smooth. Add shortening and vanilla extract and beat until combined. Slowly add in powdered sugar beating slightly between each addition. Add two tablespoons of milk and beat on medium-high for 1–2 minutes.

5. Separate buttercream into three separate smaller bowls (about 1¾ cup in each). In first bowl, add 1–2 tablespoons of milk and beat with hand whisk until at desired consistency; set aside. In second bowl, add cocoa powder and 1–2 tablespoons of milk beating with a hand whisk until at desired consistency. In third bowl, add strawberry extract, pink gel coloring, and 1 tablespoon of milk, beating with a hand whisk until at desired consistency. You will now have one vanilla, one chocolate, and one strawberry portion.

6. Once cupcakes have completely cooled, prepare 3 piping bags with large circle tips and pipe buttercreams using the flower petal technique (page 26), piping one mound of each flavor. (You can also pipe one flavor at a time, cleaning and reusing piping bag and tip.) Chill in fridge for 5 minutes and smooth out mound tops with a clean paper towel. Top with chopped peanuts and candied cherries—or real cherries— just before serving.

Orange Creamsicle

Creamsicle push pops were a favorite of mine growing up, an odd combo of orange and vanilla that works perfectly together. But we no longer have to wait for the ice cream man because these sweet swirls will do the trick-all year round!

MAKES 24–30 CUPCAKES

ORANGE CUPCAKES

1 box white cake mix

¼ cup flour

3 large eggs

12 oz. orange soda (room temperature)

orange gel coloring

CREAMSICLE BUTTERCREAM

1 cup unsalted butter

1 cup shortening

1 Tbsp. orange extract

1 tsp. vanilla extract

8 cups powdered sugar

6–8 Tbsp. milk

orange gel coloring

PARTY-PERFECT

For a festive summer display, push plain popsicle sticks down the center of the cupcakes, creating faux popsicles.

1. Preheat oven to 350 degrees. Line two 12-cup cupcake pans with cupcake liners and set aside.

2. In a medium mixing bowl, sift together cake mix and flour and set aside. In the bowl of a stand mixer (or large mixing bowl) using the paddle attachment, beat together eggs, soda, and a small amount of orange gel coloring at low speed. Add the dry ingredients and beat until just combined. If orange color is not bright enough, add small amounts of orange gel coloring until desired color is reached. Once all ingredients are incorporated, scrape the sides and bottom of the bowl and turn mixer up to medium and beat once more for 15–20 seconds. Do not overbeat.

3. Spoon three tablespoons of batter into each cupcake liner and bake on middle oven rack for 16–18 minutes, baking up to 24 cupcakes side by side at a time. (For best results, bake cupcakes one pan at a time.) Once a toothpick comes out clean, remove from oven and allow cupcakes to rest in pan for 2–4 minutes before removing and transferring to a cooling rack. Prepare pan and repeat this step with any remaining batter.

4. While cupcakes are cooling, prepare frosting. In the bowl of a stand mixer (or large mixing bowl) using the paddle attachment, cream butter at medium speed until soft and smooth. Add shortening and vanilla extract and beat until combined. Slowly add in powdered sugar, beating slightly between each addition. Add milk one tablespoon at a time, beating in between additions until at desired consistency. Turn mixer up to medium-high and beat for one minute. Remove one cup of vanilla buttercream and place it in a separate small bowl; set aside. Add orange extract and a small amount of orange gel coloring to the remaining vanilla buttercream and beat for an additional minute.

5. Once cupcakes have completely cooled, frost cupcakes with buttercreams using the two-layer effect (page 27) and a large circle tip and an open star tip.

Pink Lemonade

Nothing says summer like a cold pink lemonade or an adorable pink lemonade cupcake. They're a little sweet and a little sour—a combo we just can't resist!

MAKES 24–30 CUPCAKES

PINK LEMONADE CUPCAKES

1 box white cake mix

1 packet pink lemonade Kool-Aid

4 large egg whites

½ cup sour cream

1¼ cup milk

¼ cup melted butter (slightly cooled)

pink gel coloring (optional)

PINK LEMONADE BUTTERCREAM

1 cup unsalted butter

1 cup shortening

1 packet pink lemonade Kool-Aid

8 cups powdered sugar

pink gel coloring

6–8 Tbsp. milk

TOPPING

24–30 lemon candies

SWEET SWIRLS

To create the pink ombre frosting effect as shown, color frosting a light pink and separate into three bowls. Add a little more pink to the second bowl and twice as much to the third bowl.

1. Preheat oven to 350 degrees. Line two 12-cup cupcake pans with cupcake liners and set aside.

2. In a medium mixing bowl, sift together cake mix and Kool-Aid and set aside. In the bowl of a stand mixer (or large mixing bowl) using the paddle attachment, beat together egg whites, sour cream, and milk at low speed. Add dry ingredients and beat until just combined. Beat in melted butter until just combined. If pink color isn't strong enough, add a small amount of gel coloring. Once all ingredients are incorporated, scrape the sides and bottom of the bowl and turn mixer up to medium-high and beat once more for 30 seconds.

3. Spoon three tablespoons of batter into each cupcake liner and bake on middle oven rack for 16–18 minutes, baking up to 24 cupcakes side by side at a time. (For best results, bake cupcakes one pan at a time.) Once a toothpick comes out clean, remove from oven and allow cupcakes to rest in pan for 2–4 minutes before removing and transferring to a cooling rack. Prepare pan and repeat this step with any remaining batter.

4. While cupcakes are cooling, prepare buttercream. In the bowl of a stand mixer (or large mixing bowl) using the paddle attachment, cream butter at medium speed until soft and smooth. Add shortening and Kool-Aid and beat until combined. Slowly add in powdered sugar, beating slightly between each addition. Add two tablespoons of milk and small amounts of pink gel coloring until desired color is achieved. Then add remaining milk one tablespoon at a time, beating in between each addition until at desired consistency.

5. Once cupcakes have completely cooled, frost cupcakes with pink lemonade buttercream using traditional swirl technique (page 24) and open star tip. Top with lemon candies.

S'mores

MAKES 24–30 CUPCAKES

GRAHAM CRACKER CUPCAKE

1 box yellow cake mix

1 cup graham cracker fine crumbs

½ tsp. cinnamon

5 large eggs

½ cup sour cream

1¼ cup milk

¼ cup melted butter (slightly cooled)

CHOCOLATE GANACHE

1 cup Hershey's chocolate chips

4 Tbsp. heavy cream

MARSHMALLOW FROSTING

½ cup unsalted butter

7 oz. marshmallow fluff

2 tsp. vanilla extract

5 cups powdered sugar

¼ tsp. salt

2–3 Tbsp. milk

TOPPINGS

2 Tbsp. crushed graham cracker

24–30 small chocolate pieces

24–30 small graham cracker pieces

1. Preheat oven to 350 degrees. Line two 12-cup cupcake pans with cupcake liners and set aside.

2. In a medium mixing bowl, sift together cake mix, graham cracker crumbs, and cinnamon and set aside. Beat together eggs, sour cream, and milk at low speed. Add dry ingredients and beat until just combined. Beat in melted butter until just combined. Once all ingredients are incorporated, scrape the sides and bottom of the bowl and turn mixer up to medium and beat once more for 15–20 seconds. Do not overbeat.

3. Spoon three tablespoons of batter into each cupcake liner and bake on middle oven rack for 16–18 minutes, baking up to 24 cupcakes side by side at a time. (For best results, bake cupcakes one pan at a time.) Once a toothpick comes out clean, remove from oven and allow cupcakes to rest in pan for 2–4 minutes before removing and transferring to a cooling rack. Prepare pan and repeat this step with any remaining batter.

4. While cupcakes are cooling, prepare ganache and frosting. For ganache, microwave heavy cream for 30 seconds, using a small glass bowl. Stir in chocolate chips until almost smooth and place back in microwave for 30 seconds. Stir until smooth and then set aside to cool. To prepare frosting, cream butter at medium speed until soft and smooth. Add marshmallow fluff and vanilla extract and beat until combined. Slowly add in powdered sugar and salt, beating slightly between each addition. Add milk one tablespoon at a time, beating in between additions until at desired consistency. Turn mixer up to medium-high and beat for one minute.

5. Once cupcakes have completely cooled, pipe or spread slightly cooled chocolate ganache onto cupcakes. Pipe marshmallow frosting on top of ganache using the ruffle technique (page 24) and a jumbo circle tip. Sprinkle with graham cracker crumbs and top cupcakes with pieces of graham cracker and chocolate bar pieces.

30 40

Candy Bar

Take them to watch the game, game night at home, or
just to impress and you'll score major points.

MAKES 24–30 CUPCAKES

MILK CHOCOLATE CUPCAKES

1 box milk chocolate cake mix

4 Tbsp. instant milk chocolate pudding

4 large eggs

½ cup sour cream

1 cup milk

¼ cup melted butter (slightly cooled)

CANDY BAR FROSTING

½ cup unsalted butter

1 cup peanut butter

13 oz. marshmallow fluff

2 cups powdered sugar

3–5 Tbsp. milk

TOPPINGS

1½ cup caramel melting bits

4 Tbsp. milk

¼ cup chopped peanuts

MIX IT UP

Take these cupcakes to the next level by drizzling melting chocolate on top and sprinkling with crushed candy bar pieces.

1. Preheat oven to 350 degrees. Line two 12-cup cupcake pans with cupcake liners and set aside.

2. In a medium mixing bowl, sift together cake mix and pudding and set aside. In the bowl of a stand mixer (or large mixing bowl) using the paddle attachment, beat together eggs, sour cream, and milk at low speed. Add dry ingredients and beat until just combined. Beat in melted butter until just combined. Once all ingredients are incorporated, scrape the sides and bottom of the bowl and turn mixer up to medium and beat once more for 15–20 seconds. Do not overbeat.

3. Spoon three tablespoons of batter into each cupcake liner and bake on middle oven rack for 16–18 minutes, baking up to 24 cupcakes side by side at a time. (For best results, bake cupcakes one pan at a time.) Once a toothpick comes out clean, remove from oven and allow cupcakes to rest in pan for 2–4 minutes before removing and transferring to a cooling rack. Prepare pan and repeat this step with any remaining batter.

4. While cupcakes are cooling, prepare frosting. In the bowl of a stand mixer (or large mixing bowl) using the paddle attachment, cream butter at medium speed until soft and smooth. Add peanut butter and marshmallow fluff and beat until combined. Slowly add in powdered sugar, beating slightly between each addition. Add milk one tablespoon at a time, beating in between additions until at desired consistency. Frosting will be smooth and soft, but able to hold its shape. Turn mixer up to medium-high and beat for one minute.

5. Once cupcakes have completely cooled, frost cupcakes with candy bar frosting using traditional swirl technique (page 24), stopping halfway up. Chill cupcakes in fridge for five minutes. While chilling, prepare caramel topping. Place caramel melting bits and milk in a glass bowl and microwave for 30 seconds at a time until melted, stopping to stir in between. While still slightly warm, spoon or pipe using a decorating bottle onto the center of chilled cupcake tops. Sprinkle chopped peanuts on top of caramel.

Marshmalloween

Say "boo" this Halloween with these adorably scary treats. Monsters big and small love this fluffy marshmallow frosting and will gobble it right up. So you don't have to worry about any extras haunting you later.

MAKES 24–30 CUPCAKES

CHOCOLATE FUDGE CUPCAKES

1 box chocolate fudge cake mix

4 Tbsp. instant chocolate fudge pudding

4 large eggs

½ cup sour cream

1 cup milk

¼ melted butter (slightly cooled)

MARSHMALLOW FROSTING

½ cup unsalted butter

7 oz. marshmallow fluff

2 tsp. vanilla extract

5 cups powdered sugar

¼ tsp. salt

2–3 Tbsp. milk

MIX IT UP

Instead of using ghost toppers, turn the frosting into a little ghost by adding eyes and a mouth out of round black sprinkles or small candies.

1. Preheat oven to 350 degrees. Line two 12-cup cupcake pans with cupcake liners and set aside.

2. In a medium mixing bowl, sift together cake mix and pudding and set aside. In the bowl of a stand mixer (or large mixing bowl) using the paddle attachment, beat together eggs, sour cream, and milk at low speed. Add dry ingredients and beat until just combined. Beat in melted butter until just combined. Once all ingredients are incorporated, scrape the sides and bottom of the bowl and turn mixer up to medium and beat once more for 15–20 seconds. Do not overbeat.

3. Spoon three tablespoons of batter into each cupcake liner and bake on middle oven rack for 16–18 minutes, baking up to 24 cupcakes side by side at a time. (For best results, bake cupcakes one pan at a time.) Once a toothpick comes out clean, remove from oven and allow cupcakes to rest in pan for 2–4 minutes before removing and transferring to a cooling rack. Prepare pan and repeat this step with any remaining batter.

4. While cupcakes are cooling, prepare frosting. In the bowl of a stand mixer (or large mixing bowl) using the paddle attachment, cream butter at medium speed until soft and smooth. Add marshmallow fluff and vanilla extract and beat until combined. Slowly add in powdered sugar and salt, beating slightly between each addition. Add milk one tablespoon at a time, beating in between additions until at desired consistency. Turn mixer up to medium-high and beat for one minute.

5. Once cupcakes have completely cooled, frost cupcakes using traditional swirl technique (page 24) and a jumbo circle piping tip. Frosting will be soft but will settle and hold shape.

Poison Apple

How about a trick and a treat? This green apple frosting and devil's food cake makes the perfect costume for your not-so-toxic treats. Go ahead, have a bite…

MAKES 24–30 CUPCAKES

DEVIL'S FOOD CUPCAKES

1 box devil's food cake mix

4 Tbsp. instant chocolate pudding

4 large eggs

½ cup sour cream

1 cup milk

¼ cup melted butter (slightly cooled)

GREEN APPLE BUTTERCREAM

1 cup unsalted butter

1 cup shortening

1–2 pkg. green apple Kool-Aid

8 cups powdered sugar

6–8 tbsp. milk

lime green gel coloring (or equal parts green and yellow)

MIX IT UP

Add even more toxic effect by filling cupcakes with vanilla pudding dyed lime green.

1. Preheat oven to 350 degrees. Line two 12-cup cupcake pans with cupcake liners and set aside.

2. In a medium mixing bowl, sift together cake mix and pudding and set aside. In the bowl of a stand mixer (or large mixing bowl) using the paddle attachment, beat together eggs, sour cream, and milk at low speed. Add dry ingredients and beat until just combined. Beat in melted butter until just combined. Once all ingredients are incorporated, scrape the sides and bottom of the bowl and turn mixer up to medium and beat once more for 15–20 seconds. Do not overbeat.

3. Spoon three tablespoons of batter into each cupcake liner and bake on middle oven rack for 16–18 minutes, baking up to 24 cupcakes side by side at a time. (For best results, bake cupcakes one pan at a time.) Once a toothpick comes out clean, remove from oven and allow cupcakes to rest in pan for 2–4 minutes before removing and transferring to a cooling rack. Prepare pan and repeat this step with any remaining batter.

4. While cupcakes are cooling, prepare buttercream. In the bowl of a stand mixer (or large mixing bowl) using the paddle attachment, cream butter at medium speed until soft and smooth. Add shortening and 1 Kool-Aid packet and beat until combined. Slowly add in powdered sugar, beating slightly between each addition. Beat in two tablespoons of milk and green gel coloring until desired color is achieved. Then add remaining milk one tablespoon at a time, beating in between each addition until at desired consistency, scraping bowl in between to incorporate color evenly. If you would like even more green apple flavor add second packet of green apple Kool-Aid. Turn mixer up to medium-high and beat for 1–2 minutes.

5. Once cupcakes have completely cooled, frost cupcakes with green apple buttercream using the traditional swirl technique (page 24) and a large round tip.

Caramel Pumpkin Cheesecake

Why pick just one pumpkin when you can bake a whole patch, topped with a caramel cheesecake frosting. Hello, fall!

MAKES 30–36 CUPCAKES

PUMPKIN CUPCAKES

1 box spice cake mix

2 tsp. pumpkin pie spice

4 large eggs

2 cups pumpkin purée

1¼ cup milk

¼ cup melted butter (slightly cooled)

CARAMEL CHEESECAKE FROSTING

1 cup unsalted butter

8 oz. cream cheese

4 Tbsp. instant cheesecake pudding

1 tsp. vanilla extract

3 Tbsp. caramel topping

5 cups powdered sugar

4–6 Tbsp. milk

TOPPINGS

green sprinkles

pumpkin candies

PARTY-PERFECT

Serve this little patch of pumpkins on a tray covered in green paper shred as "grass" for a finished look. Serve alongside of green rope candy for "vines."

1. Preheat oven to 350 degrees. Line two 12-cup cupcake pans with cupcake liners and set aside.

2. In a medium mixing bowl, sift together cake mix and pumpkin pie spice and set aside. In the bowl of a stand mixer (or large mixing bowl) using the paddle attachment, beat together eggs, pumpkin purée, and milk at low speed. Add dry ingredients and beat until just combined. Beat in melted butter until just combined. Once all ingredients are incorporated, scrape the sides and bottom of the bowl and turn mixer up to medium and beat once more for 15–20 seconds. Do not overbeat.

3. Spoon three tablespoons of batter into each cupcake liner and bake on middle oven rack for 16–18 minutes, baking up to 24 cupcakes side by side at a time. (For best results, bake cupcakes one pan at a time.) Once a toothpick comes out clean, remove from oven and allow cupcakes to rest in pan for 2–4 minutes before removing and transferring to a cooling rack. Prepare pan and repeat this step with any remaining batter.

4. While cupcakes are cooling, prepare frosting. Whisk together cheesecake pudding and four tablespoons of milk in a small bowl; set aside. In the bowl of a stand mixer (or large mixing bowl) using the paddle attachment, cream butter at medium speed until soft and smooth. Add cream cheese and vanilla extract and beat until combined. Slowly add in powdered sugar, beating slightly between each addition. Add pudding mix and remaining milk one tablespoon at a time, beating in between additions until at desired consistency. Turn mixer up to medium-high and beat for 1–2 minutes.

5. Once cupcakes have completely cooled, frost cupcakes with caramel cheesecake frosting using traditional swirl technique (page 24) and an open star tip. Top with green sprinkles and pumpkin toppers if desired. Keep refrigerated in airtight container until served.

Cinnamon Maple Pecan

Fall is my favorite time to bake. I love how all of the flavors and scents of fall take over the house as the leaves change around us outside. These cupcakes will definitely get you in the spirit with hints of warm pecan, cinnamon, and maple.

MAKES 24–30 CUPCAKES

PECAN CUPCAKES

1 box pecan cake mix

4 large eggs

½ sour cream

1 cup milk

¼ cup melted butter (slightly cooled)

CINNAMON MAPLE BUTTERCREAM

1 cup unsalted butter

1 cup shortening

1 Tbsp. McCormick maple flavoring

½ Tbsp. cinnamon extract

8 cups powdered sugar

6–7 Tbsp. milk

TOPPER TIPS

For an additional topper, cut out small leaves from pie crust, sprinkle with cinnamon sugar, and bake until crisp.

1. Preheat oven to 350 degrees. Line two 12-cup cupcake pans with cupcake liners and set aside.

2. In a medium mixing bowl, sift cake mix and set aside. In the bowl of a stand mixer (or large mixing bowl) using the paddle attachment, beat together eggs, sour cream, and milk at low speed. Add cake mix and beat until just combined. Beat in melted butter until just combined. Once all ingredients are incorporated, scrape the sides and bottom of the bowl and turn mixer up to medium and beat once more for 15–20 seconds. Do not overbeat.

3. Spoon three tablespoons of batter into each cupcake liner and bake on middle oven rack for 16–18 minutes, baking up to 24 cupcakes side by side at a time. (For best results, bake cupcakes one pan at a time.) Once a toothpick comes out clean, remove from oven and allow cupcakes to rest in pan for 2–4 minutes before removing and transferring to a cooling rack. Prepare pan and repeat this step with any remaining batter.

4. While cupcakes are cooling, prepare buttercream. In the bowl of a stand mixer (or large mixing bowl) using the paddle attachment, cream butter at medium speed until soft and smooth. Add shortening, maple flavoring, and cinnamon extract and beat until combined. Slowly add in powdered sugar, beating slightly between each addition. Add milk one tablespoon at a time, beating in between additions until at desired consistency. Turn mixer up to medium-high and beat for 1–2 minutes.

5. Once cupcakes have completely cooled, frost cupcakes with cinnamon maple buttercream using the traditional swirl technique (page 24) and large circle tip. Top with premade leaf toppers and leaf sprinkles if desired.

Sugar Cookie

Making sugar cookies is such a fun holiday tradition. This year, make some new memories by adding cupcakes to those sugar cookies. Double the fun, double the yum!

MAKES 24–30 CUPCAKES

SUGAR COOKIE CUPCAKES

1 box vanilla cake mix

4 Tbsp. instant vanilla pudding

4 large eggs

½ cup sour cream

1¼ cup milk

¼ cup melted butter (slightly cooled)

sanding sugar to top

SUGAR COOKIE DOUGH FROSTING

1 cup flour

7 cups powdered sugar

Pinch of salt

2 cups unsalted butter

1½ Tbsp. butter extract

½ tsp. vanilla

6–8 Tbsp. milk

small sugar cookies to top

TOPPER TRICKS

Make simple toppers by baking 1-inch sugar cookies with small fondant cutters. For toppers in a flash, cut out small toppers from store-bought soft sugar cookies.

1. Preheat oven to 350 degrees. Line two 12-cup cupcake pans with cupcake liners and set aside.

2. In a medium mixing bowl, sift together cake mix and pudding and set aside. In the bowl of a stand mixer (or large mixing bowl) using the paddle attachment, beat together eggs, sour cream, and milk at low speed. Add dry ingredients and beat until just combined. Beat in melted butter until just combined. Once all ingredients are incorporated, scrape the sides and bottom of the bowl and turn mixer up to medium and beat once more for 15–20 seconds. Do not overbeat.

3. Spoon three tablespoons of batter into each cupcake liner and sprinkle sanding sugar on top of each cupcake liner. Bake on middle oven rack for 16–18 minutes, baking up to 24 cupcakes side by side at a time. (For best results, bake cupcakes one pan at a time.) Once a toothpick comes out clean, remove from oven and allow cupcakes to rest in pan for 2–4 minutes before removing and transferring to a cooling rack. Prepare pan and repeat this step with any remaining batter.

4. While cupcakes are cooling, prepare frosting. In a large mixing bowl whisk together flour, powdered sugar, and salt; set aside. In the bowl of a stand mixer (or additional large mixing bowl) using the paddle attachment, cream butter at medium speed until soft and smooth. Add extracts and beat until combined. Slowly add dry ingredients, beating slightly between each addition. Add milk one tablespoon at a time, beating in between additions until at desired consistency. Turn mixer up to medium-high and beat for 1–2 minutes.

5. Once cupcakes have completely cooled, frost cupcakes with sugar cookie frosting using the ruffle technique (page 26) and a large French star tip. Top with small sugar cookies if desired.

Blue Velvet Coconut

Eight days of celebration is definitely going to call for some cupcakes! Combine these winter-themed cupcakes with nine candles to create the perfect sweet menorah.

MAKES 24–30 CUPCAKES

BLUE VELVET CUPCAKES

1 box white cake mix

4 large egg whites

½ cup sour cream

1¼ cup buttermilk

blue gel coloring

¼ cup melted butter (slightly cooled)

COCONUT BUTTERCREAM

1 cup unsalted butter

1 cup shortening

3 Tbsp. coconut extract

8 cups powdered sugar

6–7 Tbsp. milk

PARTY-PERFECT

These also make great snow-themed cupcakes. Top with snowmen or snowflakes and white sanding sugar for a flurry effect.

1. Preheat oven to 350 degrees. Line two 12-cup cupcake pans with cupcake liners and set aside.

2. In a medium mixing bowl, sift cake mix and set aside. In the bowl of a stand mixer (or large mixing bowl) using the paddle attachment, beat together egg whites, sour cream, buttermilk, and a small amount of blue gel coloring at low speed. Add cake mix and beat until just combined. Beat in melted butter until just combined. If blue color isn't bold enough, add a little more blue coloring. Once all ingredients are incorporated, scrape the sides and bottom of the bowl and turn mixer up to medium and beat once more for 15–20 seconds. Do not overbeat.

3. Spoon three tablespoons of batter into each cupcake liner and bake on middle oven rack for 16–18 minutes, baking up to 24 cupcakes side by side at a time. (For best results, bake cupcakes one pan at a time.) Once a toothpick comes out clean, remove from oven and allow cupcakes to rest in pan for 2–4 minutes before removing and transferring to a cooling rack. Prepare pan and repeat this step with any remaining batter.

4. While cupcakes are cooling, prepare buttercream. In the bowl of a stand mixer (or large mixing bowl) using the paddle attachment, cream butter at medium speed until soft and smooth. Add shortening and coconut extract and beat until combined. Slowly add in powdered sugar, beating slightly between each addition. Add milk one tablespoon at a time, beating in between additions until at desired consistency. Turn mixer up to medium-high and beat for 1–2 minutes.

5. Once cupcakes have completely cooled, frost cupcakes with coconut buttercream using traditional swirl technique (page 24) and a jumbo circle tip.

Mocha Peppermint Crunch

Peppermint everywhere is a sure sign of winter! Let your cupcakes get in on the craze with these fluffy peppermint swirls on top of a coffee-infused cake with peppermint crunch mixed in.

MAKES 24–30 CUPCAKES

MOCHA CUPCAKES

1 box chocolate fudge cake mix

¼ cup flour

4 large eggs

½ cup sour cream

1 cup coffee (slightly cooled)

¼ cup melted butter (slightly cooled)

½ cup crushed peppermint

PEPPERMINT BUTTERCREAM

1 cup unsalted butter

1 cup shortening

2 Tbsp. peppermint extract

½ Tbsp. vanilla extract

8 cups powdered sugar

6–8 Tbsp. milk

red gel coloring

TOPPING

¼ cup crushed peppermint

TOPPER TIPS

Tiny candy canes and pieces of peppermint bark make great alternative toppers.

1. Preheat oven to 350 degrees. Line two 12-cup cupcake pans with cupcake liners and set aside.

2. In a medium mixing bowl, sift together cake mix and flour and set aside. In the bowl of a stand mixer (or large mixing bowl) using the paddle attachment, beat together eggs, sour cream, and coffee at low speed. Add dry ingredients and beat until just combined. Beat in melted butter until just combined. Once all ingredients are incorporated, scrape the sides and bottom of the bowl and turn mixer up to medium and beat once more for 15–20 seconds. Do not overbeat. Fold in crushed peppermint.

3. Spoon three tablespoons of batter into each cupcake liner and bake on middle oven rack for 16–18 minutes, baking up to 24 cupcakes side by side at a time. (For best results, bake cupcakes one pan at a time.) Once a toothpick comes out clean, remove from oven and allow cupcakes to rest in pan for 2–4 minutes before removing and transferring to a cooling rack. Prepare pan and repeat this step with any remaining batter.

4. While cupcakes are cooling, prepare buttercream. In the bowl of a stand mixer (or large mixing bowl) using the paddle attachment, cream butter at medium speed until soft and smooth. Add shortening and extracts and beat until combined. Slowly add in powdered sugar, beating slightly between each addition. Add milk one tablespoon at a time, beating in between additions until at desired consistency. Turn mixer up to medium-high and beat for 1–2 minutes.

5. Once cupcakes have completely cooled, frost cupcakes with peppermint buttercream using the traditional swirl technique (page 24) and a large circle tip. Use the painted stripe effect (page 27) to create the peppermint look. Sprinkle crushed peppermint on top of cupcakes to finish.

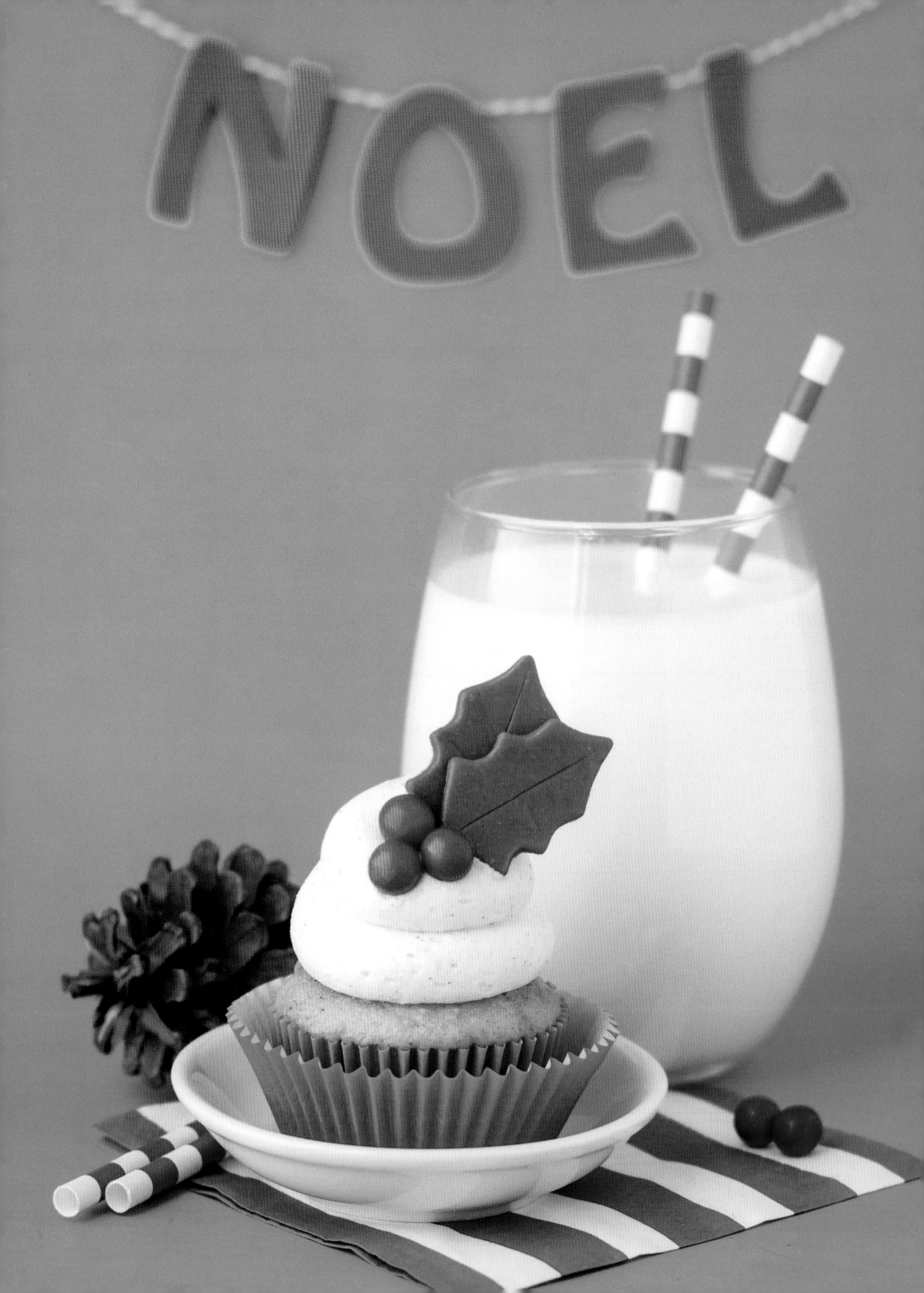
NOEL

Cinnamon Eggnog

Deck the halls with this favorite holiday-drink-turned-cupcake.
You'll be sure to fa-la-la-la-la!

MAKES 24–30 CUPCAKES

EGGNOG CUPCAKES

1 box French vanilla cake mix

1 tsp. cinnamon

½ tsp. nutmeg

4 Tbsp. instant French vanilla pudding

4 large eggs

½ cup sour cream

1¼ cups eggnog

¼ cup melted butter (slightly cooled)

EGGNOG BUTTERCREAM

1 cup unsalted butter

1 cup shortening

½ tsp. vanilla extract

½ tsp. rum extract (optional)

8 cups powdered sugar

1 tsp. cinnamon

½ tsp. nutmeg

8–10 Tbsp. eggnog

TOPPER TIPS

To create these holly toppers, cut out leaves from green fondant and let dry. Add red Sixlets to finish.

1. Preheat oven to 350 degrees. Line two 12-cup cupcake pans with cupcake liners and set aside.

2. In a medium mixing bowl, sift together cake mix, cinnamon, nutmeg, and pudding and set aside. In the bowl of a stand mixer (or large mixing bowl) using the paddle attachment, beat together eggs, sour cream, and eggnog at low speed. Add dry ingredients and beat until just combined. Beat in melted butter until just combined. Once all ingredients are incorporated, scrape the sides and bottom of the bowl and turn mixer up to medium and beat once more for 15–20 seconds. Do not overbeat.

3. Spoon three tablespoons of batter into each cupcake liner and bake on middle oven rack for 16–18 minutes, baking up to 24 cupcakes side by side at a time. (For best results, bake cupcakes one pan at a time.) Once a toothpick comes out clean, remove from oven and allow cupcakes to rest in pan for 2–4 minutes before removing and transferring to a cooling rack. Prepare pan and repeat this step with any remaining batter.

4. While cupcakes are cooling, prepare buttercream. In the bowl of a stand mixer (or large mixing bowl) using the paddle attachment, cream butter at medium speed until soft and smooth. Add shortening and extract(s) and beat until combined. Slowly add in powdered sugar, cinnamon, and nutmeg, beating slightly between each addition. Add eggnog one tablespoon at a time, beating in between additions until at desired consistency. Turn mixer up to medium-high and beat for 1–2 minutes.

5. Once cupcakes have completely cooled, frost cupcakes with eggnog buttercream using the traditional swirl technique (page 24) and jumbo circle tip.

Cookies & Cream

You're going to need a cupcake with enough sparkle to bring in the New Year, and these, I assure you, will do the job! As one of my most requested cupcakes, they might even become a yearly tradition.

MAKES 24–30 CUPCAKES

CHOCOLATE FUDGE CUPCAKES

1 box dark chocolate fudge cake mix

4 Tbsp. instant chocolate pudding

4 large eggs

½ cup sour cream

1 cup milk

¼ cup melted butter (slightly cooled)

30 sandwich cookies

COOKIES & CREAM FROSTING

4 cups heavy whipping cream

2 (.35-oz) packets of whipped cream stabilizer

12 Tbsp. powdered sugar

4–5 Tbsp. crushed cookie

TOPPER TIPS

Why not create a little more noise for the celebration? Top these cupcakes with tiny confetti poppers for a little more "pop!"

1. Preheat oven to 350 degrees. Line two 12-cup cupcake pans with cupcake liners. Twist off the tops of 24 cookies and place one, cookie-cream-side up, in the bottom of each cupcake liner and set aside. In a food processor or Ziploc bag, finely crush leftover cookie tops and set aside. (Save leftover cookies for additional cupcakes.)

2. In a medium mixing bowl, sift together cake mix and pudding and set aside. In the bowl of a stand mixer (or large mixing bowl) using the paddle attachment, beat together eggs, sour cream, and milk at low speed. Add dry ingredients and beat until just combined. Beat in melted butter until just combined. Once all ingredients are incorporated, scrape the sides and bottom of the bowl and turn mixer up to medium and beat once more for 15–20 seconds. Do not overbeat.

3. Spoon three tablespoons of batter into each cupcake liner (on top of cookie) and bake on middle oven rack for 16–18 minutes, baking up to 24 cupcakes side by side at a time. (For best results, bake cupcakes one pan at a time.) Once a toothpick comes out clean, remove from oven and allow cupcakes to rest in pan for 2–4 minutes before removing and transferring to a cooling rack. Prepare pan and repeat this step with any remaining batter.

4. While cupcakes are cooling, prepare frosting. Place large metal mixing bowl and electric whisk attachment(s) into freezer to chill. Once cold, remove chilled bowl from freezer and beat heavy whipping cream until stiff peaks have formed. Add in powdered sugar and vanilla extract and beat once more, just until combined. Fold in crushed cookie crumbs.

5. Once cupcakes have cooled, frost cupcakes with cookies and cream frosting using the traditional swirl technique (page 24) and open star tip. Top with some remaining crushed cookie crumbs. Store in an airtight container and refrigerate until served.

Sweet Sources

CUPCAKE SUPPLIES

Baking Cups

Simply Baked
www.simplybaked.us

Candy Flavorings

Lorann
lorannoils.com

Gel Colorings

Americolor
www.americolorcorp.com

Wilton
www.wilton.com

Greaseproof Cupcake Liners & Paper Straws

Sweets & Treats Boutique
shopsweetsandtreats.com

Piping Tips

Wilton
www.wilton.com

Ateco
www.atecousa.com

Sprinkles & Edible Decorations

Country Kitchen SweetArt
www.countrykitchensa.com

Layer Cake Shop
www.layercakeshop.com

Wilton
www.wilton.com

Fondant

Satin Ice
www.satinice.com

Candy Toppers

Party City
http://www.partycity.com

CRAFT & BAKING STORES

Piping Bags, Gel Coloring, Cutters & Sprinkles

Country Kitchen SweetArt
www.countrykitchensa.com

Joann
www.joann.com

Michaels
www.michaels.com

Hobby Lobby
www.hobbylobby.com

PACKAGING

Baker's Twine

The Twinery
thetwinery.com

Cupcake Containers & Boxes

Country Kitchen SweetArt
www.countrykitchensa.com

PHOTOGRAPY

Author Head Shot

Sonia Boukaia
www.soniaboukaia.com

PRESENTATION

Cupcake Stadium Stand

Cake Pop Stand Co.
www.cakepopstandco.com

Napkins, Garlands, Dishes & Styling Items

Target
www.Target.com

The Cherries on Top

To My Husband—To my biggest fan, sweetest encourager, and best friend. Without you, none of this would be possible. Thank you for always being you, for pushing me to follow my dreams when they seem impossible, for encouraging me when I need it most, and for putting up with countless cake mix runs, endless sprinkles, crazy ideas, late night coffee refills, and painfully consuming more cupcakes than is possible to count. You are simply amazing—the sprinkles to my cupcake. And you know how much I love sprinkles!

To My Girls—Cadence, Miley, and Bailey, thank you for being the sweetest inspiration there is, for making me giggle when I need it most, for waiting patiently to eat cupcakes after pictures, and for pushing me to be the best mommy I can be. But most of all, thank you for forever reminding me that life is short but sweet. No matter where you go or what you do, always let those little lights shine.

To My Parents—Mom and Dad, thanks for always being there for me from the start, for raising me in a home together and surrounded by love, and for showing me what true love, commitment, hard work, and family really mean. Thank you for encouraging me to embrace creativity even if there's still paint on the walls and glitter on the table to prove it.

To My Family—Thank you for always being there to cheer me on and standing behind me with the best support system a girl could ask for. From test-baking recipes, sharing my work, putting up with my enthusiasm, and simply believing in me, it means the world.

To My Friends & Army Family—To Shar, Tabitha, Nicole, you guys are amazing. Thank you for being there from the start, for seeing me through my crazy dreams, and for being the best taste testers there are and the most amazing friends a girl could ask for. To Angela, thank you for being there through thick and thin no matter what and for understanding, nurturing, and challenging my passion. You saw so much more for me than I ever imagined, and inspired me to rise to the occasion! To Nancy and Jenny, who have been the most helpful friends a girl could ask for, never hesitating for a moment to help throughout this process. Thank you for being there every step of the way without complaint. From helpful hands to endless testing, I am so grateful. To Callye, my sweet friend and blogger idol, I am forever grateful for your endless encouragement and your willingness to obsess over details right along with me. I can only hope to one day return the favor. To Lynlee, I can honestly say without you, this unrealized dream would have never taken flight! You were encouraging *Cupcakery* from the very moment it came alive, and I am so thankful to have had you along this sweetly swirled journey.

To Shannon of Sweets & Treats Boutique— Thank you for supplying the endless amounts of adorably awesome grease-proof cupcake liners, paper straws, and printed bags used throughout *Cupcakery*. This book wouldn't be the same without your incredible products and dedicated friendship.

To Janine of Cake Pop Stand & Co.—You didn't hesitate for even a moment when I asked you to create a whole new stadium stand just for my candy bar cupcakes (page 125). You took a simple idea and made it incredible. Thank you so much; I love my new stand!

To Hannah and the Cedar Fort Team—The best editors around! Thank you for taking me on this journey and making it the smoothest one possible, for being excited right along with me, for encouraging my creativity, for answering my endless questions, and for never once second-guessing my vision. Thank you!

To the Cupcakery Test Bakers—To Wendell, Alex, Tabitha, Jaclyn, Brittany, Jessica, Jenny, Nicole, Virginia, Gail, Tiffany, and Lynnette. Thanks for taking the time to create the recipes within *Cupcakery* to help me ensure each recipe was simple and sweet!

To the Readers of MBC—Last, but certainly not least. Thank you for giving me a place to inspire, for allowing me to share a small part of your sweet celebrations, and for always being there with support, encouragement, and excitement. You followed along with my greatest—and not-so–great—ideas no matter the outcome! You guys are incredible. I truly wish I could thank each and every one of you by name. Without you, this sweet reality would be just a dream.

Index

A

Almond Wedding Cake 85

B

Banana Cream Pie 61
Banana Taffy 81
Blueberry-Stuffed French Toast 42
Blue Raspberry 78
Blue Velvet Coconut 137
Bubble Gum 70

C

Cake Batter 82
Candy Bar 125
Caramel Popcorn 77
Caramel Pumpkin Cheesecake 130
Cherry Almond Flowers 109
Cherry Cheesecake 62
Cherry Cola 53
Chocolate Caramel Irish Cream 102
Chocolate Confetti 89
Chocolate Malt 57
Cinnamon Eggnog 141
Cinnamon Maple Pecan 133
Cinnamon Roll 45
Cookies & Cream 142
Cotton Candy 74

D

Dirt Pudding 73

F

Frosting, chocolate buttercream 21
Frosting, vanilla buttercream 21

G

German Chocolate Coconut Almond 105
Grape Soda 50
Green Velvet Butterscotch 101

I

Ice Cream Sundae 58

L

Lemon Pudding 106

M

Marshmalloween 126
Mint Chocolate 113
Mocha Peppermint Crunch 138
Mocha Swirl 46
Monster Cookie Dough 65

N

Neapolitan 117

O

Orange Creamsicle 118

P

Patriotic Apple Pie 114
PB & J 69
Pineapple Cream 86
Pink Lemonade 121
Poison Apple 129

R

Red Velvet Cheesecake 98
Root Beer Float 54

Cooking Measurement Equivalents

Cups	Tablespoons	Fluid Ounces
⅛ cup	2 Tbsp.	1 fl. oz.
¼ cup	4 Tbsp.	2 fl. oz.
⅓ cup	5 Tbsp. + 1 tsp.	
½ cup	8 Tbsp.	4 fl. oz.
⅔ cup	10 Tbsp. + 2 tsp.	
¾ cup	12 Tbsp.	6 fl. oz.
1 cup	16 Tbsp.	8 fl. oz.

Cups	Fluid Ounces	Pints/Quarts/Gallons
1 cup	8 fl. oz.	½ pint
2 cups	16 fl. oz.	1 pint = ½ quart
3 cups	24 fl. oz.	1½ pints
4 cups	32 fl. oz.	2 pints = 1 quart
8 cups	64 fl. oz.	2 quarts = ½ gallon
16 cups	128 fl. oz.	4 quarts = 1 gallon

Other Helpful Equivalents

1 Tbsp.	3 tsp.
8 oz.	½ lb.
16 oz.	1 lb.

Metric Measurement Equivalents

Approximate Weight Equivalents

Ounces	Pounds	Grams
4 oz.	¼ lb.	113 g
5 oz.		142 g
6 oz.		170 g
8 oz.	½ lb.	227 g
9 oz.		255 g
12 oz.	¾ lb.	340 g
16 oz.	1 lb.	454 g

Approximate Volume Equivalents

Cups	US Fluid Ounces	Milliliters
⅛ cup	1 fl. oz.	30 ml
¼ cup	2 fl. oz.	59 ml
½ cup	4 fl. oz.	118 ml
¾ cup	6 fl. oz.	177 ml
1 cup	8 fl. oz.	237 ml

Other Helpful Equivalents

½ tsp.	2½ ml
1 tsp.	5 ml
1 Tbsp.	15 ml

About the Author

Toni's sweet adventure began with her love for parties and creative knack. What started as a hobby of self-taught home cake baking and decorating quickly grew into a successful baking blog and a love for all things adorably sweet. Her work can be found on many websites and publications around the world, including *Better Homes and Gardens*, *Good Housekeeping*, Today, Yahoo!, and more. Toni is currently residing in Texas with her husband, Ben; three girls, Cadence, Miley, and Bailey; and their dog, Sprinkles.

Find lots more of Toni's recipes, tutorials, creative projects, and more at www.makebakecelebrate.com.